of prayer with

SAINT FRANCIS OF ASSISI

15 days
of prayer series

On a journey, it's good to have a guide. Even great saints took spiritual directors or confessors with them on their itineraries toward sanctity. Now you can be guided by the most influential spiritual figures of all time. The 15 Days of Prayer series introduces their deepest and most personal thoughts.

This popular series is perfect if you are looking for a gift, or if you want to be introduced to a particular guide and his or her spirituality. Each volume contains:

- ∞ A brief biography of the saint or spiritual leader
- ∞ A guide to creating a format for prayer or retreat
- ∞ Fifteen meditation sessions with focus points and reflection guides

15 days
of prayer with
SAINT FRANCIS OF ASSISI

THADDÉE MATURA, o.f.m

TRANSLATED BY
PAUL LACHANCE, o.f.m.

NEW CITY PRESS
Hyde Park, NY

Published in the United States by New City Press
202 Cardinal Rd., Hyde Park, NY 12538
www.newcitypress.com
©2009 New City Press (English translation)

This book is a translation of *Prier 15 Jours avec François d'Assise*,
published by Nouvelle Cité, Montrouge, France.

Cover design by Durva Correia

Library of Congress Cataloging-in-Publication Data:

Matura, Thaddée.
  [Prier 15 jours avec François d'Assise. English]
  15 days of prayer with St. Francis of Assisi / by Thaddée Matura ;
translated by Paul Lachance.
      p. cm.
  Includes bibliographical references.
  ISBN 978-1-56548-315-6 (pbk. : alk. paper) 1. Francis, of Assisi,
Saint, 1182-1226—Meditations. 2. Spiritual life—Catholic Church.
I. Title. II. Title: Fifteen days of prayer with St. Francis of Assisi.
  BX2179.F64E5 2009
  269'.6—dc22   2008053418

Printed in the United States of America

Contents

How to Use
This Book

A n old Chinese proverb, or at least what
I am able to recall of what is supposed
to be an old Chinese proverb, goes something
like this: "Even a journey of a thousand miles
begins with a single step." When you think
about it, the truth of the proverb is obvious.
It is impossible to begin any project, let alone
a journey, without taking the first step. I think
it might also be true, although I cannot recall
if another Chinese proverb says it, "that the
first step is often the hardest." Or, as someone
else once observed, "the distance between a
thought and the corresponding action needed
to implement the idea takes the most energy."
I don't know who shared that perception with
me but I am certain it was not an old Chinese
master!

With this ancient proverbial wisdom, and the
not-so-ancient wisdom of an unknown contem-

porary sage still fresh, we move from proverbs to presumptions. How do these relate to the task before us?

I am presuming that if you are reading this introduction it is because you are contemplating a journey. My presumption is that you are preparing for a spiritual journey and that you have taken at least some of the first steps necessary to prepare for this journey. I also presume, and please excuse me if I am making too many presumptions, that in your preparation for the spiritual journey you have determined that you need a guide. From deep within the recesses of your deepest self, there was something that called you to consider Saint Francis of Assisi as a potential companion. If my presumptions are correct, may I congratulate you on this decision? I think you have made a wise choice, a choice that can be confirmed by yet another source of wisdom, the wisdom that comes from practical experience.

Even an informal poll of experienced travelers will reveal a common opinion; it is very difficult to travel alone. Some might observe that it is even foolish. Still others may be even stronger in their opinion and go so far as to insist that it is necessary to have a guide, especially when you are traveling into uncharted waters and into territory that you have not yet experienced. I am of the personal opinion that a traveling companion is welcome under all circumstances. The thought of traveling alone, to some exciting destination without someone to share the journey with does not capture my imagination or channel my enthusiasm. However, with that being noted, what is simply a matter of preference on the normal journey becomes a matter of necessity when a person embarks on a spiritual journey.

The spiritual journey, which can be the most challenging of all journeys, is experienced best with a guide, a companion, or at the very least, a friend in whom you have placed your trust. This observation is not a preference or an opinion but rather an established spiritual necessity. All of the great saints with whom I am familiar had a spiritual director or a confessor who journeyed with them. Admittedly, at times the saints might well have traveled far beyond the experience of their guide and companion but more often than not they would return to their director and reflect on their experience. Understood in this sense, the director and companion provided a valuable contribution and necessary resource. When I was learning how to pray (a necessity for anyone who desires to be a full-time and public "religious person"), the community of men that I belong to gave me a great gift. Between my second and third year in college, I was given a one-year sabbatical, with all expenses paid and all of my personal needs met. This period of time was called novitiate. I was officially designated as a novice, a beginner in the spiritual journey, and I was assigned a "master," a person who was willing to lead me. In addition to the master, I was provided with every imaginable book and any other resource that I could possibly need. Even with all that I was provided, I did not learn how to pray because of the books and the unlimited resources, rather it was the master, the companion who was the key to the experience.

One day, after about three months of reading, of quiet and solitude, and of practicing all of the methods and descriptions of prayer that were available to me, the master called. "Put away the books, forget the method, and just listen." We went into a room, became quiet, and tried to recall the presence of God, and then, the master simply prayed out loud and permitted me to listen to his prayer. As he prayed, he revealed his hopes, his dreams, his struggles, his successes, and most of all, his relationship with God. I discovered as I listened that his prayer was deeply intimate but most of all it was self-revealing. As I learned about him, I was led through his life experience to the place where God dwells. At that moment I was able to understand a little bit about what I was supposed to do if I really wanted to pray.

The dynamic of what happened when the master called, invited me to listen, and then revealed his innermost self to me as he communicated with God in prayer, was important. It wasn't so much that the master was trying to reveal to me what needed to be said; he was not inviting me to pray with the same words that he used, but rather that he was trying to bring me to that place within myself where prayer becomes possible. That place, a place of intimacy and of self-awareness, was a necessary stop on the journey and it was a place that I needed to be led to. I could not have easily discovered it on my own.

The purpose of the volume that you hold in your hand is to lead you, over a period of fifteen days or, maybe more realistically, fifteen prayer periods, to a place where prayer is possible. If you already have a regular experience and practice of prayer, perhaps this volume can help lead you to a deeper place, a more intimate relationship with the Lord.

It is important to note that the purpose of this book is not to lead you to a better relationship with Saint Francis of Assisi, your spiritual companion. Although your companion will invite you to share some of his deepest and most intimate thoughts, your companion is doing so only to bring you to that place where God dwells. After all, the true measurement of all companions for the journey is that they bring you to the place where you need to be, and then they step back, out of the picture. A guide who brings you to the desired destination and then sticks around is a very unwelcome guest!

Many times I have found myself attracted to a particular idea or method for accomplishing a task, only to discover that what seemed to be inviting and helpful possessed too many details. All of my energy went to the mastery of the details and I soon lost my enthusiasm. In each instance, the book that seemed so promising ended up on my bookshelf, gathering dust. I can assure you, it is not our intention that this book end up in your bookcase, filled with promise, but unable to deliver.

There are three simple rules that need to be followed in order to use this book with a measure of satisfaction.

Place: It is important that you choose a place for reading that provides the necessary atmosphere for reflection and that does not allow for too many distractions. Whatever place you choose needs to be comfortable, have the necessary lighting, and, finally, have a sense of "welcoming" about it. You need to be able to look forward to the experience of the journey. Don't travel steerage if you know you will be more comfortable in first class and if the choice is realistic for you. On the other hand, if first class is a distraction and you feel more comfortable and more yourself in steerage, then it is in steerage that you belong.

My favorite place is an overstuffed and comfortable chair in my bedroom. There is a light over my shoulder, and the chair reclines if I feel a need to recline. Once in a while, I get lucky and the sun comes through my window and bathes the entire room in light. I have other options and other places that are available to me but this is the place that I prefer.

Time: Choose a time during the day when you are most alert and when you are most receptive to reflection, meditation, and prayer. The time that you choose is an essential component. If you are a morning person, for example, you should choose a time that is in the morning. If you are more alert in the afternoon, choose an afternoon time slot; and if evening is your preference, then by all means choose the evening. Try to avoid "peak" periods in your daily routine when you know that you might be disturbed. The time that you choose needs to be your time and needs to work for you.

It is also important that you choose how much time you will spend with your companion each day. For some it will be possible to set aside enough time in order to read and reflect on all the material that is offered for a given day. For others, it might not be possible to devote one time to the suggested material for the day, so the prayer period may need to be extended for two, three, or even more sessions. It is not important how long it takes you; it is only important that it works for you and that you remain committed to that which is possible.

For myself I have found that fifteen minutes in the early morning, while I am still in my robe and pajamas and before my morning coffee, and even before I prepare myself for the day, is the best time. No one expects to see me or to interact with me because I have not yet "announced" the fact that I am awake or even on the move. However, once someone hears me in the bathroom, then my window of opportunity is gone. It is therefore important to me that I use the time that I have identified when it is available to me.

Freedom: It may seem strange to suggest that freedom is the third necessary ingredient, but I have discovered that it is most important. By freedom I understand a certain "stance toward life," a "permission to be myself and to be gentle and understanding of who I am." I am constantly amazed at how the human person so easily sets himself or herself up for disappointment and perceived failure. We so easily make judgments about ourselves and our actions and our choices, and very often those judgments are negative, and not at all helpful.

For instance, what does it really matter if I have chosen a place and a time, and I have missed both the place and the time for three days in a row? What does it matter if I have chosen, in that twilight time before I am completely awake and still a little sleepy, to roll over and to sleep for fifteen minutes more? Does it mean that I am not serious about the journey, that I really don't want to pray, that I am just fooling myself when I say that my prayer time is important to me? Perhaps, but I prefer to believe that it simply means that I am tired and I just wanted a little more sleep. It doesn't mean anything more than that. However, if I make it mean more than that, then I can become discouraged, frustrated, and put myself into a state where I might more easily give up. "What's the use? I might as well forget all about it."

The same sense of freedom applies to the reading and the praying of this text. If I do not find the introduction to each day helpful, I don't need to read it. If I find the questions for reflection at the end of the appointed day repetitive, then I should choose to close the book and go my own way. Even if I discover that the reflection offered for the day is not the one that I prefer and that the one for the next day seems more inviting, then by all means, go on to the one for the next day.

That's it! If you apply these simple rules to your journey you should receive the maximum benefit and you will soon find yourself at your destination. But be prepared to be surprised. If you have never been on a spiritual journey you should know that the "travel brochures" and the other descriptions that you might have heard are nothing compared to the real thing. There is so much more than you can imagine.

A final prayer of blessing suggests itself:

> Lord, catch me off guard today.
> Surprise me with some moment of
>   beauty or pain
> So that at least for the moment
> I may be startled into seeing that you
>   are here in all your splendor,
> Always and everywhere,
> Barely hidden,
> Beneath,
> Beyond,
> Within this life I breathe.

Frederick Buechner

Rev. Thomas M. Santa, CSsR
Liguori, Missouri

Abbreviations

Adm	The Admonitions
BlB	Blessing for Brother Bernard
BlL	Blessing for Brother Leo
CtC	Canticle of the Creatures
CtExh	Canticle of Exhortation for the Ladies of San Damiano
LtAnt	A Letter to Brother Anthony of Padua
LtCl	A Letter to the Clergy
LrCus	A Letter to the Custodians
1LtF	The First Letter to the Faithful
2LtF	The Second Letter to the Faithful
LtL	A Letter to Brother Leo
LtMin	A Letter to a Minister
LtOrd	A Letter to the Entire Order
LtR	A Letter to Rulers of the Peoples

ExhP	Exhortation to the Praise of God
PrOF	A Prayer Inspired by the Our Father
PrsG	Praises of God
PrCr	The Prayer before the Crucifix
OfP	The Office of the Passion
ER	The Earlier Rule
LR	The Later Rule
RH	A Rule for Hermitages
SalBVM	A Salutation of the Blessed Virgin Mary
SalV	A Salutation of the Virtues
Test	The Testament
TPJ	True and Perfect Joy

Translations from the writings of Saint Francis, with occasional corrections, are from *The Saint* (Francis of Assisi: Early Documents, vol. 1), eds. R. Armstrong, J. A. Hellmann, W. Short (New York: New City Press, 1999).

I would like to thank Suzanne Haraburd, Dick and Nancy Cusack, Colette Wisnewski for reviewing my translation and making helpful suggestions. The focus points and questions were written in collaboration with Colette Wisnewski.

Chronology

*T*his brief chronology is taken from Pierre Brunette, *Francis and His Conversions*, translated by Paul Lachance, O.F.M. and Kathryn Krug (Quincy Il.: Franciscan Press, 1977), xi–xiii.

1181   Birth of Francis, son of Peter Bernadone and Lady Pica in Assisi. He is baptized John in the church of San Rufino, renamed Francis by his father upon his return from a trip to France.

1195–96 At the age of 14 or 15, Francis oficially enters the trade of his father, a cloth merchant, becoming a member of the Corporation of Merchants.

1198   Destruction of the Rocca Maggiore fortress in Assisi by the townspeople. Francis participates in the uprising and later collaborates in the restoration of the fortress. He learns the rudiments of masonry.

1199   Civil war in Assisi. The city is eman-
            cipated and becomes a Commune.
            Beginnings of the conflicts, which
            last until 1209, with the neighboring
            city of Perugia.

1202   Battle of Ponte San Giovanni between
            Assisi   and   Perugia   (November).
            Francis takes part in the battle and is
            imprisoned in Perugia for a year. Onset
            of his ill health.

1203   Francis is ransomed and returns to
            Assisi seriously ill.

1204   Long convalescence: inner changes.

1205–06   Military campaigns in Apulia: Francis
            joins the Crusade of the papal army
            (Spring 1205). Health relapse on the
            way to Spoleto. A vision commands
            him to return home. Francis' progres-
            sive withdrawal from the company of
            his friends and worldly life. Intervals
            of solitude and prayer. He serves the
            lepers and spends time with the poor.
            At San Damiano, he hears a call from
            the Cross and begins a stint as a man-
            ual laborer by restoring the chapel.
            He adopts the hermit's garb. Sale of
            the cloth at the fair in Foligno. Start
            of the conflict with his father.

1206		Francis' trial before Bishop Guido as demanded by his father (Spring). Renunciation of his worldly belongings. The bishop takes him under his wings.

1206–08	Ongoing work as penitent-mason: restoration of the churches of San Damiano, San Pietro, and Santa Maria degli Angeli (Portiuncula).

1208		Francis hears the Gospel of the feast of St. Matthias (February, 24). He becomes aware of his vocation: to live as a disciple of Jesus. Start of preaching and itinerancy in the vicinity of Assisi. Within a few months the first companions arrive (Bernard, Peter, Giles, and others). First missions outside of Umbria (Spring).

1209		The first twelve brothers present themselves before Pope Innocent III. Francis had written a brief "form of life." Oral approval by the pope (Spring).

1209–10	The brothers settle in at the Portiuncula, the mother church of the Order of the Friars Minor. Communal period: organization into provinces, convening of the brotherhood in "chapters," establishment of obligatory novitiate, the place of studies, preaching and missions, formulation of the life plan, etc.

1220   Francis' return from a trip to the East. Internal difficulties in the Order. Francis renounces his post as Minister General, designates Peter of Catanii as his successor. At Francis' request, Rome names Cardinal Hugolino as protector of the Order.
Rapid deterioration of his health (ophthalmitis, ulcers, fevers, dropsy). Repeated Admonitions and Letters sent to the brothers and various categories of people (the faithful, rulers, clerics, etc.).

1221   General Chapter (May 30). The Earlier Rule is written.

1223   Redaction of the Later Rule, discussed at a Chapter, approved by a Bull of Honorius III (November 29). Christmas celebration in the grotto at Greccio.

1224   Saint Michael's Lent at Mount La Verna. On or about the feast of the

Exaltation of the Cross, Francis receives the stigmata of the Passion.

1225   Worsening of Francis' physical condition. He is treated by cauterization of his ophthalmitis. Sojourn at San Damiano, he experiences the dark night of the soul. Composition of the *Canticle of Creatures* in the aftermath of a quarrel between the *podestà* of Assisi and the bishop. Another treatment for his eye ailment.

1226   Redaction of his Testament; death of Francis at the Portiuncula on October 3; burial at the church of Saint George.

1228   Francis is canonized by his friend Hugolino, now Pope Gregory IX.

1229   Transportation of his body to the crypt of the new basilica built in his honor.

Introduction

Francis: His Image and Message

*D*oes spending fifteen days with Francis (1182–1226) mean we will get to know his extraordinary life, be amazed over it, and draw some inspiration from it for our personal behavior? Given his fascinating figure, one is tempted to think this will happen, thus identifying his image with his message.

In the pages that follow we are choosing a different approach. Francis has left us a message which is distinct from his person, one addressed to his contemporaries, but also to men and women of all ages. This message does not propose his personal example, but rather traces a path nurtured by the Gospel and available to all believers. Francis' call to the men and women of today is contained in his writings. Francis is a "spiritual writer."

Francis, A "Spiritual Writer"?

To speak of Francis as a spiritual writer surprises. Is he not, rather, someone unclassifiable, a person without formal education, hardly knowing how to read and write Latin, the "official" language of the era?

And yet, by this man, "ignorant and unlettered," as he refers to himself on a few occasions, a solidly based tradition has retained some thirty written texts of varying length, an anthology consisting of some hundred pages. Even two hand-written texts have been preserved on bits of parchment. In comparison, St. Dominic, his contemporary and a learned cleric, has left practically no text of any significance. All Francis' texts, except for two (*The Canticle of the Creatures* and *The Exhortation to Poor Ladies*) composed in the Umbrian dialect are written in a very simple and at times incorrect Latin.

This anthology, which is comprised of many literary genres (poems, rules, letters, prayers), nonetheless has a great unity of spirit, style, and above all, content. These are not disconnected pieces of writing. One feels that a powerful personality is behind them. With a poverty of means, the writings succeed in saying, or better still, felicitously suggesting, the basic components of every human life which is receptive to the Gospel.

Francis was keenly aware of the importance of his writings. He considered them as "the very words of Jesus Christ and the words of the Holy Spirit." He insists that they be read, memorized and copied so that they may be made known to others. He addresses his message to men and women of every walk of life "which are and will be," of every age and place. Strangely enough, down through the centuries, this message has not received the attention that it deserves.

Piously preserved and transcribed — as testified by the existence of several hundred manuscripts between the thirteenth and fifteenth century — Francis' texts did not begin to be seriously studied as the main and basic source of his spiritual vision until these past fifty years. It is as if Francis' image — celebrated, enlarged, and idealized by ancient and modern hagiography — had obfuscated his message, the object of which is neither his person nor his particular spiritual journey. These writings give us hardly any information on Francis — which is the object of hagiographical studies — but they enable us to see his conception of God, humankind, and his way of understanding life according to the Gospel.

In this respect, these writings are of irreplaceable value in enabling us to glimpse that which inspired Francis' life and thus to introduce us to the very sources of Franciscan spirituality.

Francis, A Master of the Spiritual Life

At first glance, Francis' texts seem atemporal. Not only is Francis himself rarely mentioned, but the turmoil of the early thirteenth century in which they are rooted is only faintly echoed. Beyond some concrete attitudes proposed to Christians and to the brothers (radical poverty, work, mendicancy), and which are very much of their time, the focus is always on the deep underlying basis of human existence. These texts are evangelical in the sense that, like the Gospels, they touch upon something eternal and permanent in the human condition including its miserable aspect, loved as it is by God and called to fullness of life. In other words, Francis' writings are essentially spiritual ones revealing to men and women the face of God as well as their own, and inviting them to follow in the footsteps of Christ in poverty and joyfulness.

The main source, very explicitly emphasized, from which Francis draws his inspiration as well as the spiritual and doctrinal content of his themes, is the Scriptures of the Old and New Testament as mediated by the liturgy. Some of his texts are but a long patchwork of biblical citations judiciously selected and forming a coherent whole.

These few indices suffice to enable us to detect in Francis a true spiritual master although one of a particular genre, to be sure, for he is a lay person without any formal schooling. Except for some of the Fathers of the Desert whose sayings have been reported — apothegms — and many of whom, indeed, did not possess a theological culture, there is no male figure of this type in the Christian tradition. Francis' personality is closer to that of some of the medieval women such as Angela of Foligno or Catherine of Siena, both unlettered, or, in our day, to someone like Thérèse of Lisieux, than to doctors and scholars such as Augustine, Bernard, or John of the Cross.

But because he is simple, because he retells the Gospel for us without being too marked by a particular era and its culture, his message reaches us more easily than that of great figures: he comes across as real and relevant to our concerns.

The texts presented and commented upon here do not directly concern Francis, his life, and his achievement. Instead they propose a spiritual journey: discovery of self, the neighbor, and above all, the mystery of the Triune God, the center of every Christian life. Texts *by* Francis and not texts *on* Francis will accompany us during these fifteen days.

Fifteen Days with Francis

The fifteen days of prayer which we will spend with Francis are meant to serve as an initiation to his spiritual vision. We have selected and commented upon a certain number of his writings as a kind of anthology. The presentation and the way of articulating these texts are obviously arbitrary. Nonetheless, we believe they rightfully belong to Francis' own perspective.

With him we get started on our journey, praying to God to enlighten the darkness of our hearts (*1st day*). The light of God will initially reveal to us what it means to be part of the human condition (*2nd day)* and how the path of the most high poverty leads to true joy (*3rd day*). Furthermore, it will enable us to see everyone as a brother or sister worthy of love (*4th day*), even if they be the greatest sinners (*5th day*).

After which turning his gaze towards God, Francis proposes a spiritual journey (*6th day)* to follow and explains the meaning of a pure heart, one which "*does not cease to adore and to see the Lord God*" (*7th day*). Thereafter unfolds a grandiose vision for us to contemplate: the Father and his works (*8th day*); the mystery of Jesus, the Word of the Father (*9th day*); Mary, the Glorious Lady, and the saints (*10th day*); finally, the beauty with which God adorns all creatures, our sisters *(11th day*).

Going even deeper, Francis describes what is true spiritual knowledge: that by which the Spirit enables us to see the Father and the Son in their divine being (*12th day*). Then, from his heart — and from ours — will spring forth awe, wonderment, and pure praise (*13th day*). Afterwards, a passionate invitation, addressed to all men and women, will orient us towards "*the one thing necessary: the desire for and the pleasure of God*" (*14th day*). The culmination of the journey will consist in not holding back anything for ourselves, but to render everything back to God in thanksgiving (*15th day*).

The reader who possesses only an anecdotal acquaintance of Francis, based on the biographies, will no doubt be astonished by the density of the spiritual message of his writings. It is a *theological* message, strongly centered on the mystery of God as Trinitarian communion and on the human person as inseparable from this mystery. Francis' approach is not subjective, describing the repercussions of God's work in the soul and its human psychological effects; rather, it is *objective*, treating, from a certain distance, what is. His vision is *mystical,* according to the meaning which this word had among the Fathers of the Church. It is a vision which contemplates and reveals the *mystery of God* as he is in himself and in his work of which humankind represents the summit; it does not pay attention to subjective psychological descriptions. We will notice, also, that the spirituality is *doxological*; that is, it does not find expression in a language that is abstract and dry, but rather as a song of praise and in a poetic style.

1
The Journey Begins

Focus Point

//////////////

We are created by love for love. At key turning points of our lives, we may be at a loss on what to do to follow God's call. We do well, like Francis, to acknowledge the darkness that is in our hearts and to turn to the cross of Christ for light and guidance. To then obey the promptings of God for conversion opens our lives to a great and wonderful adventure. A good thing to remember, God's ways are not our ways and many surprises await us.

//////////////

Most high,
glorious God
enlighten the darkness of my heart
and give me

true faith,
certain hope,
and perfect charity,
sense and knowledge,
Lord,
that I may carry out
Your holy and true command.

(PrCr)

///////////////

*T*he first and no doubt the oldest of Francis' writings which has come down to us is a prayer which belongs at the beginning of his spiritual journey. He has just broken away (ca.1206) from his previous way of life, one filled with ambition and ease, but he does not know yet which path God is calling him to follow. In an abandoned chapel into which he has wandered in search of light, Francis discovers a large icon of the Crucified represented in the glory of his passion. The face is serene, the eyes are wide open, and above his head the hand of the Father is already lifting him into the heavens of the Ascension. This is the first encounter between Glory and Obscurity: the radiance of the One reveals the darkness of the other.

The prayer which then rises from Francis' heart, a prayer which he must have repeated, memorized, and later transmitted to his brothers, is a prayer for a departure, the beginning of a journey. It concerns everyone who is on a quest. And who isn't?

It is a brief, very simple text, almost banal at first glance. Yet in looking at it more closely, meditating on it, and making it one's own, its density is discovered.

At the center, dominating the entire scene, the face of *God, the most high and glorious Lord,* imposes itself. The hidden mystery, when it gradually reveals itself to men and women, initially discloses its majestic splendor. He is *God*: a generic name to designate that which is incomprehensible and unnamable; he is *Lord*: the One before whom men and women perceive themselves as dependent and subservient; he is most high or *sovereign*, in the heights and in himself inaccessible, yet radiating splendor; he is *glorious* and shines magnificently. But this vision which could frighten and scare us away is tempered by the words which follow: *enlighten, give.* The dazzling glare of God's majesty does not blind: rather it diffuses a tender light which causes joy and consoles us. The One who is called the unnamable God, the Lord, is good and generous to us: he can and wants to give what we, as supplicants, ask for.

For behold, facing this power and glory — which is God in himself even if under the aspect of the Crucified in the exalted state — is a heart filled with darkness: *the darkness of my heart.* The *heart* is the most central and deepest part of the person. It is the unifying center from which springs forth and in which converges all the desires and forces which constitute the person; it is the identity and the truth of everyone in their most personal and incommunicable aspect. But this center of gravity, the ultimate depth of the person and the force which propels us along, is shrouded with darkness.

What are these *darknesses of the heart*? One can discern within the person three concentric zones. The first is constituted of ignorance of the true self, that is, who one really is in the eyes of God. Men and women are unaware of their extraordinary grandeur: being made in God's image and that of his Son made flesh, both in one's soul and body (Adm 5). Men and women are likewise unaware of the extreme poverty of their being, their limitations, and dependency stemming from the fact of not being God. This lack of awareness of who we truly are, our blindness to our incomparable dignity as well as to our inexpressible littleness — this is one of the zones of darkness that shrouds the heart.

This initial darkness concerns the human being as a creature, an inextricable mixture of nobility and insignificance. There is another zone of darkness, one with a moral connotation. It consists of the murky world of evil which inhabits every human heart. In fact, it is "from the heart that all evil comes," as the Lord says in the Gospel (Mk 7:21), a quotation which Francis cites on a number of occasions (ER 22,7; 2LtF 37). What is at the center of the person, the heart, often resembles a marsh swarming with destructive, deadly tendencies and impulses both for oneself and for others. When men and women consent to act out these destructive impulses, the result is the darkness of evil and sin; this darkness is likewise found in every human life, even the most upright in appearance.

There is a third zone of darkness which is not knowing which path one has to follow to respond to a call which has risen from the depths, a call which comes, in fact, from God. What must I do at such a turning point in my life? To be sure, I cannot turn back, or stand still, but what indeed is the path that needs to be taken in order to be truly myself, to fulfill all the dimensions of who I am in myself and in God? The Gospel offers a few clues and markers, but it does not tell me what I must choose in order to be faithful.

But I am not condemned to darkness. The glorious Lord, before whom I stand, radiates with splendor. His sovereign light can dispel the darkness into which my heart is plunged. This light, the true one, is "our Lord Jesus Christ" (2LtF 66). Through his merciful gaze on my darkness, my own reality is unfolded, brought to light. To be able so to see what is in me and around me is already the onset of grace.

Once blindness is healed, we no longer fumble along in obscurity. Now that the path is cleared, we must get started on the journey. The prayer, henceforth, becomes more precise, more detailed:

> *give me*
> *true faith,*
> *certain hope,*
> *perfect charity,*
> *sense and knowledge.*

Among the five points requested in the prayer some are classical, some are new. The mention of the three theological virtues already proposed by St. Paul (1 Thes 1:3), which the Church beseeches in its liturgical prayer (sixteenth Sunday in ordinary time) and with which Francis identifies God himself (PrsG 6), might seem an almost banal evocation. Two new mysterious terms are associated with them: sense and knowledge. A spiritual effort is required if we are not to sidestep what we might too quickly suppose we already know.

What is a *true faith* if not an accurate vision of what is real in God's plan and just as, gradually, it takes shape in each one's story. To go beyond what is superficial, and perhaps deceptive, in order to discover in each person the living presence of a personal Love; at the same time, to see the value as well as the calling and the destiny of each person. To catch a glimpse, in a word, who God is and how his glory and passion for everyone fill the earth and the heavens — this is what is meant by a true faith.

A realistic faith also enables us to see a world in gestation: unfinished, wounded, wherein evil is far too present and expectation of happiness too uncertain. *A certain hope* which the prayer asks for consists of a bounding optimism and vitality, the certitude that God's promises and commitments cannot fail, that the absolute future — the fullness of life and happiness — is in store for those whom God loves: all men and women as well as the world as cosmos and history. It is the assurance that *a kingdom is prepared for us since the beginning of the world* (Mt 25:34; ER 23, 4) in *the happy company and eternal joy* of God (OfP).

A vision which is full and correct, an expectation which is assured and joyful, is rendered possible, and not illusory, because of *perfect charity.* This term is often understood in too limited a way; one initially thinks of it as our love for God. The New Testament revelation of charity (*Agape*) is first of all the manifestation of God's unconditional love for men and women. The only perfect charity is the overflowing, extreme, even excessive passion which burns in God's heart whose secret and fiery life in communion blazes forth to enkindle all of his creation of which men and women are the crowning achievement. To ask for perfect charity is to ask for, above all, the overwhelming revelation and receptivity to this love. It is only afterwards that a return movement is awakened in the human heart: a boundless thanksgiving, a response which is directed toward both God and human-kind, and the source of which eternally springs forth from the very heart of the Trinity.

And, as if these three gifts did not suffice, Francis asks God to complement them with *sense and knowledge*. What is this mysterious sense which seems required for these three vir-tues to fully perform their role in the journey undertaken? *Sense* here means the experience, what takes hold and seizes us as a result of what we have just discovered and glimpsed. The vision, the expectation, even the revelation of love are affirmed and transmitted by words which express concepts and images. But it does not suffice to hear, to understand intellectually, to have only a head-knowledge of what is being said. True knowledge incorporates experience, perception, a living contact and entry into the realities evoked. To have sense of in the realm of faith means to catch a glimpse of, to touch in a way, even if only obscurely and fleetingly, the object of the vision and the expectation.

But this spiritual sense (contact, experience) is not simply a blind, unsayable and inexpress-ible feeling: it is accompanied by *knowledge*, which is also asked for in the prayer, and which means intellectual clarity. One must note here that when, in his writings, Francis speaks of prayer as a movement of the heart towards God, he usually couples the word heart with that of *mens*, which indicates the human spirit in its intellectual dimension or, more simply put, the light of knowledge.

The pilgrim now is ready to depart, equipped with the viaticum necessary for the journey: five loaves of bread which, as a beggar, he or she has beseeched from the Lord of glory whose love and generosity he or she is familiar with, in spite of his or her own darknesses and poverty.

More needs to be said. The heart now enlightened, the path clearly traced, new energies released: faith, hope, love, experience and clear vision — all these require commitment, doing, action. The orant asks for and receives these manifold gifts *in order to fulfill the holy and true commands* of God.

For Francis, this commandment was surely the inner call which he had perceived (*to repair the Church*), although without being able to grasp immediately the full implication which would unfold later on in his life. But if we go beyond the historical context to make the prayer contemporary, we must ask: what is this *commandment* called holy and true, which we must carry out? For us, as for Francis himself, the simple expression *your commandment* in the singular, spontaneously brings to mind the first of all the commandments, that of the love of

God and neighbor (Mk 12:29–31) on which the whole Law is based and the prophets as well (Mt 22:40).

Thus the virtues and the experiences which have been bestowed are granted for the purpose of meeting the great and only requirement: to love God and one's neighbor with all one's being. This *royal* commandment (Jas 2:8) which encompasses and fulfills everything and has no limits (Rom 13:8), is truly *the greatest and the first* (Mt 22:38).

It is in the service of this commandment, to put it into practice in real life, that the dynamisms described above have been asked for and granted. For Francis, as for every spirituality derived from him, *doing,* as testified by the ample use of the term in his writings, is the criteria for the truth of every commitment.

This commandment of love is qualified as *holy and true.* It is *holy,* astonishing, other, different from what we ordinarily see and do. This commandment is also *true* because as it opens our hearts to receive and give love, it introduces us to the truth of ourselves. Created by and for true love, we are only fully ourselves when we allow ourselves to be grasped and moved by its dynamism. It is then that we are in the truth and liberated by an exigency that is truthful.

Thus a personal prayer, conceived by Francis at a difficult and lengthy stage of his conversion, remains relevant today for everyone who begins a journey to seek and to find God and themselves. The darknesses of the heart gradually yield as one is exposed to the radiance of divine glory; with light also comes the necessary energies to see clearly and commit oneself. The royal road of love becomes more precise. For those who take it, there opens up a great and beautiful adventure.

Reflection Questions

In the spiritual life we are always at the beginning. Right now how would you evaluate who you really are before God, your faith, your hope, your charity? Become aware of the moments of God's presence in your life and try to describe these moments. What did they feel like? What is now in the darkness of your heart? What is the light that you seek? What does standing before Christ on the cross mean to you?

2
The Wonders and Woes of the Human Condition

Focus Point

///////////

One of the challenges of the spiritual life is to truly believe that we are created body and soul in the image of God. This love of God is the source of our being able to love and accept ourselves as we are and to love and accept others as they are, an acceptance rooted both in our strengths and our weaknesses. It is an inability to love ourselves — an unlived life — and to love others that leads to the ongoing crucifixion of Christ in our world and ultimately results in structural sin and violence such as racism, famine and wars.

///////////

Consider, O human being
in what great excellence the Lord God has
placed you,

for He created and formed you to the image
*   of His beloved Son*
according to the body,
and to His likeness
according to the Spirit.
All creatures under heaven
serve, know and obey their Creator,
each according to its own nature,
better than you.
Even the demons did not crucify Him,
but you, together with them,
have crucified Him
and are still crucifying Him
by delighting in vices and sins.
In what, then, can you boast?

(Adm 5)

///////////

*T*his text from the 5th Admonition begins
with the joyful cry of a human being who
discovers himself to be the work of God, a work
that has succeeded admirably. Through a gaze
that is prolonged and ecstatic, men and women
are invited to consider the incredible heights in
which God has placed them. The body — and
here Francis is original — is formed in the image
of the body of the Son of God made human. In
modeling Adam and Eve, God had imprinted on
them the traits of the body of the One who was
to come: his Son Jesus. But the same holds true
for every human body. My body today repro-

duces the body of the first-born of all creation
(Col 1:15), and my spirit is made in the likeness
of the Father and the Son. It is to me that the
invitation is addressed once again: *Consider, O
human being, in what great excellence the Lord God
has placed you.*

The great excellence of the human person in
the totality of his or her being, body and spirit,
is based on the love that dwells in the heart of
God who has wanted as a partner a being similar
to himself although radically different. Human
beings, as St. Clare will write, are *the most worthy
of all creatures*; even when they turn away from
God and show themselves to be *ungrateful and
evil, God did and does everything good for them and
just as he has created and redeemed them, he will save
them by his mercy alone* (ER 23, 8).

We must always keep in mind this extremely
positive vision of the human person as the
image of God, willed as such from the beginning, and remaining so, even when through *our
fault, we fall* and degrade ourselves. What follows in the text after this glorious tribute, does,
in fact, pass a rather harsh judgment on our
behavior as humans.

For all creation under heaven: animal, veg-
etable, mineral, as well as the world in its totality, serve, know, and obey their creator. This is a
strange and unusual affirmation. How can these
beings which have neither intelligence nor freedom, know, serve, and obey God? Could this be

just a poetic expression without any foundation in reality? Or is it not, rather, a deep and accurate intuition of the mysterious laws to which all that exists must conform itself?

After this enthusiastic and kindly glance at the subhuman world, where already we find the initial sketches of what will later become the *Canticle of the Creatures,* comes a very unfavorable comparison towards the human person: this world submits itself to and obeys God better than we do! Even if humans are the only ones who are intelligent and free, we are also the only ones who do not integrate themselves into the harmony of the marvelous plan that God has foreseen and proposed for his glory, as well as for our complete happiness. We are the only ones who can elude it and pursue another path, one leading to who knows what kind of abyss ...

> *Even the demons did not crucify Him,*
> *but you, together with them,*
> *have crucified Him*
> *and are continuing to crucify Him*
> *by delighting in vices and sins.*

This passage which is quoted in the *Catechism of the Catholic Church* (n. 598) makes our case as humans even worse. All creation serves, knows and obeys God better than we humans do. This is certainly a reproach, even if nuanced, because it is not universally applicable. Humans also serve, know, and obey. But what Francis is

accusing men and women of is extremely serious. We have crucified and continue to crucify
the Creator. Jesus the crucified man is identified,
without any transition, with the Lord God, the
Creator. Strangely enough, the demons are not
the main ones responsible for Christ's murder.
They seem rather to be mere accomplices in a
crime for which the initiative comes from men
and women.

Francis boldly breaks down the time barrier.
He addresses men and women of all ages and each
one of us today. I was there at the moment of the
crucifixion as a responsible agent; still today, my
sin continues the Passion. To be sure, the partici-
pation is not a material one; rather it is in *delighting in vices and sins* that I crucify the Lord.

To delight in vices and sins means, in Francis'
language, to turn in on ourselves with the illusion
of being self-sufficient and capable of building
up our personality by ourselves, when in reality
we are sapping away our true substance at the
expense of not only ourselves, but also of others
and of God. Sin is not merely the transgression of
an arbitrary law which would put us in a state of
legal infraction against God. If sin wounds God,
if it crucifies his Son, it is because it ravages and
destroys us the sinners. God cannot bear that we
who are his image and beloved from all eternity
be degraded. The self-destruction, unconscious to
be sure, of the sinner caught in the complicated
and enticing net of *his vices* is a form of suffer-

ing which affects God as much as and even more than humans. *To crucify the Lord* (with the complicity of demons ...) means to inflict an incurable wound, that of a love refused and not shared, on "the One who loves us and has washed away our sins by his blood" (Rev 1:5).

In what, then, can you boast?

One could respond to this question by saying that our glory as humans lies in our being made according to the image and likeness of God, the Father and the Son, which is affirmed so vigorously by Francis. However, at stake here are not the gifts received but the deeds which should flow from them. That which is deficient in our deeds, our sin, and the cause of the death of Love, cannot be made up for either by knowledge, beauty, wealth, or even by the gift of miracle working.

> *For if you were so skillful and wise*
> *that you possessed all knowledge,*
> *knew how to interpret every kind of language*
> *and to scrutinize heavenly matters with skill:*
> *you cannot boast in these things.*
>
> *(Adm 5)*

One can detect in this passage reminiscences from St. Paul when he speaks of the various charisms and their subordination to love (1 Cor 12:28; 13:2). Francis knows and enumerates the multiple facets of knowledge: intellectual acumen (*skillful*); life experience and good judgment (*wisdom*); various forms of *knowledge*, to which is added, or so it seems, spiritual gifts; language interpretation and theological insight (*scrutinize heavenly matters*). The one who possesses these values, presented as they are here, cannot boast in them, for the demons themselves possess forms of knowledge superior to human beings:

> *For one demon knew about heavenly matters*
> *and now knows more about those of earth*
> *than all human beings....*
> *In the same way, even if you were more*
> *handsome and richer than*
> *Everyone else, and even if you worked miracles*
> *so that you put demons to flight:*
> *all these things are contrary to you;*
> *nothing belongs to you;*
> *you can boast of none of these things.*
>
> *(Adm 5)*

After knowledge, other values, acknowledged as positive, are highlighted: physical beauty (the only time that Francis speaks about it, and he seems to appreciate it) and wealth, that is to say possessions: whatever falls into the category of having. At the summit appears the gift of working miracles, which includes the capacity to chase demons away as did the apostles (Lk 10:17–20). But in the same way that the Lord, in Luke's gospel, warned his disciples not to rejoice in the fact that demons are subject to them — this capacity belongs to God alone — Francis, likewise, in an almost brutal fashion, will repeat:

> *all these things are contrary to you;*
> *nothing belongs to you;*
> *you can boast of none of these things.*

Nothing belongs to you is the statement that is the most striking in this passage. All that men and women have received and continue to receive from God: intellectual qualities, physical beauty and strength, spiritual gifts, all are part of our make-up. We, nonetheless, are not to claim ownership of what we have received, as if we were totally autonomous and independent. Men and women are like a brook that flows as long as the spring continues to feed it. With keen spiritual insight, Francis touches the very root of our capacity to sin: no longer to perceive ourselves as a work of God, as a gift received from and dependent upon God, but rather to claim this gift as our own, to retain it jealously, to see ourselves as owners and to boast of it. This no doubt corresponds to a temptation which he experienced in himself and in other spiritual persons: to flaunt as one's own gifts coming from beyond oneself in order to find acceptance by God, others, and oneself.

The tender, kind, and fraternal Francis pushes us, men and women, against the wall, strips us of all pretense, empties us and leaves us naked. And the response he gives to the question raised previously leaves us flabbergasted:

But we can boast: in our weaknesses
and in carrying each day the holy cross
of our Lord Jesus Christ.

(Adm 5)

Francis has understood that the only reality that, strictly speaking, belongs to us as human beings is our condition as creatures, which makes us limited, ephemeral, mortal, and capable of evil. To boast in this means to accept this fact, acknowledge ourselves as poor and as beggars, and through this be open and receptive to the merciful tenderness of God; all the more so because of the heaviness of the multiple forms of human poverties, this cross so heavy for us to carry, we do not carry it alone. It has become *the holy cross* since God himself, in the person of his son Jesus, has taken it upon himself, assuming in all ways the human condition.

Reflection Questions

What is your self-image? Are you capable of truly loving yourself body and soul? What relationships do you see between loving God, loving yourself and loving your neighbor? How do you find the proper balance? Are we aware that it is our sins, our failures to love, that contribute to the ongoing crucifixion of Christ in the world? What does it mean to "boast in your weaknesses"?

3
Perfect Joy

Focus Point

//////////////

Our culture's plan for happiness is a life without sacrifice and suffering. The Gospel proposes the redemptive value of suffering and the discovery of true joy in the midst of trial and suffering, a discovery rooted in God. It is not based on power, prestige and/or success. It is not superficial or sentimental. Its paradox is that it emerges out of rejection, persecution and abandonment.

//////////////

One day at Saint Mary's, blessed Francis
   called Brother Leo
And said: "Brother Leo, write."
He responded: "Look I'm ready!"
"Write," Francis said, "what true joy is."

A messenger arrives and says
that all the Masters of Paris have entered
    the Order.
Write: this isn't true joy!
Or, that all the prelates, archbishops and
    bishops beyond the mountains,
as well as the King of France and the King
    of England
have entered the Order.
Write: this isn't true joy!
Again, my brothers have gone to the non-
    believers
and converted all of them to the faith;
or, I have so much grace from God
that I heal the sick and perform miracles. I
tell you true joy doesn't consist in any of
    these things.

                                            (TPJ)

/////////////

*T*his famous text is known in its longer
version as found in the *Fioretti* (ch. 8), a
version which amplifies and romanticizes the
narrative to the extent of making us forget the
hard message it contains. The text we comment
upon here is shorter and simpler. Critics tell us
that it is Francis' original dictation rather than
the edifying and poetic development of it which
came later.

What is true joy and where can one find it? This is a question which bothers every human being. Joy, a serene and deeply contented heart, the silent radiance of happiness, how can one attain it? Once again, Francis gives us a paradoxical response. Joy is not to be found where an initial and superficial experience may lead us to think it can be found. Its hidden source is revealed only after having been dredged out, as it were, by trials.

Francis first of all tells us where true joy is not to be found. He doesn't even stop at the description of false and fleeting joys which he handily dismisses in his twentieth admonition: *idle and empty words which lead people to laughter.* The joys described in this text, joys which he and the brothers could have experienced upon the spectacular expansion of the Order, were legitimate. Who would not rejoice over the gospel conversion, the option for a radically poor life, which would be chosen by the intellectual, ecclesial and even civic circles of thirteenth century society? As imaginary and rhetorical as the narrative may seem, it nonetheless corresponds, in part, to reality. There were indeed masters of the University of Paris (Alexander of Hales), church administrators, and even kings who were touched by the spiritual movement unleashed by Francis. *Beyond the mountains*: France, England, Paris, and Oxford were affected by the movement as much as and perhaps even more than

Italy. In France and England, there were strong sympathies with, and at times outright adherence to, the Franciscan movement. But even if all these wonderful and influential people had in fact made a serious commitment to the Order founded by Francis, this would not, in spite of the justifiable pride (an ambiguous one ...) that could be derived from it, constitute true joy.

The text goes on to envision situations more overtly religious, this time deeds by brothers and supernatural charisms that Francis himself would have received. To go to the at the time considered unbelievers (Muslims), avoid every form of quarreling and proselytizing, be submissive to all and confess that they are Christians, is the mission which Francis assigns to his brothers, as they await the day when they might proclaim the faith (ER 16). If, impossible as it may sound, this great mass of people adhered to the Gospel, what a happy event that would be, what a grace! And yet, this still would not constitute true joy.

After those who are outside the Order: university masters, bishops, kings, and after the brothers, Francis puts himself at center stage, as if the experience of joy concerned him personally. He imagines himself (but is it only imagination?) having received extraordinary graces from God: the gift of healing as well as an unlimited gift of working other types of miracles. The one who is granted such a grace is surely close to God, even a friend of God; such a one would find cause therein to rejoice. This is not denied; and yet, like a bolt from the blue, the affirmation returns and is extended to cover everything preceding it: *I tell you true joy does not consist in any of these things.*

> *"Then, what is true joy?"*
> *I return from Perugia and arrive here in the dead of night.*
> *It's winter time, muddy and so cold that icicles have formed*
> *on the edges of my habit and keep striking my legs*
> *and blood flows from such wounds.*
> *Freezing, covered with mud and ice, I come to the gate and,*
> *after I've knocked and called for some time, a brother comes and asks: "Who are you?"*
> *"Brother Francis," I answer.*
> *"Go away!" he says. "This is not a decent hour for wandering about!*
> *You may not come in!"*
>
> *When I insist, he replies: "Go away! You are simple and stupid! Don't come back to us again! There are many of us here like you — we don't need you!"*
> *I stand again at the door and say: "For the love of God, take me in tonight!" And he replies:*

*"I will not! Go to the Crosier's place and
ask there!"*

*I tell you this: If I had patience and did not
become upset,
true joy, as well as true virtue and the salvation of my soul
would consist in this.*

(TPJ)

The question *what is true joy* bounces back. Suspense mounts as the response is given only gradually. In the first part, positive reasons are given for rejoicing: the spiritual success of the Order, the missionary conquests, personal charisms — all to be immediately discarded. Now that the motivations for true joy are finally indicated, it is paradoxically the somber and pain-ful dimensions of existence which are depicted.

In the background of the declaration on *true joy, as well as true virtue and the salvation of the soul*, lies the experience of a winter night wherein one is so muddied and cold that icicles form at the edge of one's habit and keep striking at the legs so that blood flows from the wounds. In this bleak setting the wanderer is hastening towards a hostel. Behind the anecdote, there lies an image of the human condition: a person lost in the night, deprived of every human warmth, aversely affected by what is happening to him, an orphan and alone, yet in search of true joy.

The goal is at hand: the familiar entrance to the dwelling where live brothers who know him by name. Muddied and frozen, he repeatedly but confidently knocks on the door. That which would enable him to no longer feel alone, transform the coldness of the night into warm daylight, is a fraternal reception, or to use Francis' expression, the manifestation of a *maternal* one. But in this case, it is useless to identify himself by using his name, *Brother Francis,* or to make an appeal to the brother's sense of fraternity. The first refusal is justified by a pretext; it is late and you have not obeyed the rules. But this motivation hides another, one more basic and infinitely more painful: in the final analysis, we have no need of you; we are numerous, well qualified and have all that we need; you are very simple, someone without any culture or education; just another homeless man.

Nonetheless, the wanderer at the door does not give up. According to his custom, he appeals to what is greatest and most sacred, or so he thinks, to his brothers: the love of God. In the dead of a desolate night, faced with a refusal walled in by egotism, these two words, like a golden sunrise, can light an immense blaze capable of melting all resistance. *Take me in this night.* Nothing doing. The refusal is final. The dispatching to a leprosarium, by which the brother thought he could rid himself of his guilt, is, in a way, irreparable. Francis is identified by his brothers with the untouchable leper and, like him, excluded and marginalized. For his brothers, he no longer exists.

Here we touch the depths of poverty and solitude. The atmosphere is bleak. The repeated efforts to renew human contact, and to break the hardness of hearts by an appeal for hospitality, have failed. What remains then of true joy? Can we still speak of it when everything sinks into an unfathomable night?

> *I tell you this: if I had patience and did not become upset,*
> *true joy, true virtue and the salvation of my soul would consist of this.*

True joy and true virtue and even salvation would lie in being patient, in not becoming upset. At first glance, one has to picture an almost stoic stance before what is happening: the one who can endure the night, the cold and, above all, the rejection of his own companions without becoming upset and remaining calm and at peace, such a person could draw from this a certain awareness of his inner strength — his virtue — and rejoice in this capacity inwardly. But such a reading would not be faithful to Francis' vision and experience.

It is not the courageous and patient bearing of trials which allows us to rejoice. This would be relying on oneself, on one's successes and one's virtues — which Francis resolutely discards. Rather it is the trial, so dramatically portrayed in our narrative, which reveals what is in the person. If we are rooted in God and aware of the Love of God which surrounds us, then trials can befall us, even make us cry out and lament and yet something deeper and calmer sustains us; we can endure these trials without being destroyed. It is not the endurance of suffering that engenders joy, but it is joy, already there, which permits us to endure suffering. *Regardless of what we have to suffer in this world we maintain peace of spirit and body, because of the love of our Lord Jesus Christ* (Adm 15).

For those who have, too quickly perhaps, read and enjoyed this famous passage on perfect joy, and have let themselves be charmed by its light and poetic character, our reading of it will no doubt be surprising. For this text is of utmost gravity: true joy, the one that is deepest and most unshakable, finds, if not its source and its roots, at least its unfolding and its manifestation against the backdrop of inevitable suffering.

True joy, true virtue and salvation of the soul are granted only to those who *have followed the Lord in tribulation and persecution, in shame and hunger, in weakness and temptation and in other things; and for all these things they received eternal life from the Lord* (Adm 6). This is the harsh and wonderful lesson which Francis gives us.

Reflection Questions

What are the moments in your life when you experienced suffering, rejection, abandonment? What role did such moments play in your spiritual journey? Are you aware of the redemptive value of suffering? In what ways have you been tempted to be satisfied with a superficial, sentimental understanding of what constitutes true joy?

4
The True Brother

Focus Point

When we feel abandoned by God, we need to be aware that it is in such moments that the Good Shepherd most actively seeks us. This presence of the one who lays down his life for us is ongoing until the end of time. It is also the model for our relationships with others and community, a model that excludes all power and domination and extends itself to all whether friend or foe.

*Let us have recourse to Jesus as to the
  shepherd and guardian of our souls
  (1 Pt 2:25), who says: "I am the Good
    Shepherd who feeds my sheep
    and I lay down my life for my sheep"
    (cf. Jn 10:14-15).
All of you are brothers. Do not call anyone
    on earth your father,*

you have but one Father in heaven.
  Do not call yourselves teachers,
you have but one teacher in heaven
    (Mt 23:8–10).
If you remain in me and my words remain
    in you, ask for whatever you want and it
    will be done for you (Jn 15:7).
Wherever two or three are gathered together
    in my name, there am I in the midst of
    them (Mt 18:20). Behold I am with you
    until the end of the world (Mt 28:20).
The words I have spoken to you are spirit
and life (Jn 6:63). I am the way, the truth
and the life (Jn 14:6).

(ER 22, 32–40)

/////////////

*E*ven though all these texts are taken from the Gospels they, nonetheless, also come from Francis. He is the one who selected them, regrouped them according to a certain logic, and subsequently integrated them into his Rule (ER 22, 32–40) as the basis for his conception of community. Drawn from various sources (the Gospels of Matthew and John, Peter's first letter), they might seem loosely and artificially put together, but an attentive reading reveals their strong organic unity.

The figure of Christ as the Good Shepherd, an image of which Francis is especially fond, occupies center stage. He stands in the middle, reveals his identity, one which is always relevant: a love until death (*lays down his life for his sheep* ...) for he never ceases to tend the sheep that he leads to pasture. It is to this figure, radiant with kindness and tenderness, that we are invited to turn to so that we too become like a flock gathered around its shepherd and guardian.

Those who make up such a group create a fraternal community of equals among themselves. Among the great founders of religious orders, Francis is the only one to quote in his Rule the gospel passage which excludes the designations of *father* and *teacher.* In the community assembled around Christ — and this includes every church community whether lay or religious — there is to be neither father nor teacher other than the Father in heaven and Christ, the only teacher. It is noteworthy that in his writings the word he uses the most often after that of *Lord* is *brother.* Among themselves believers are fundamentally equal and are to behave themselves as brothers and sisters. The word and the reality of being a brother or a sister imply a common origin, equality, and a family spirit based on a certain tenderness. *Brother*, *fraternity* are terms which are dear to the Franciscan tradition. Francis is the first one in history to give the name *fraternity* to his religious group. The consciousness of fraternity is so strong in him that he will apply the names brother and sister to all of creation.

What follows in the text will take up again, on
different levels, the theme of the Lord's presence
to his community. To come to the Shepherd, to
hold oneself close to him, is already an indica-
tion of the strong cohesiveness of the community, but this cohesiveness has even deeper roots.
One must dwell not only near the Shepherd,
but within him, in him, according to the deep
Johannine meaning of these terms. Then, in
turn, the Word which is seed and breath will
dwell in us, and we, the community, will have
the joyous certitude that our true desires and
requests will be heard and granted. Like a leit-
motiv, the two following texts insist on the presence of Christ everywhere where two or three
are gathered in his name, a presence guaranteed
to last forever. The community of believers
is the place for this presence; it is by the presence of Christ and because of it that the community exists and is able to maintain itself. To
the theme of presence are associated the words
which the Lord proclaims and through which
he makes promises and demands. These words
are spirit and life: by coming to dwell among his
faithful, taking hold in them, they prevent them
from standing still and becoming settled. Like
the blowing of the wind (spirit ...) these words
stir the waters and ultimately make the attentive
hearer come alive.

The final text makes us return our gaze
towards *Jesus, shepherd and guardian*; it is meant

to emphasize strongly his central place in this sketch of the mystery of community: he is its *way, truth and life*.

By means of a collage of biblical texts Francis has just presented us with a deep vision of the community which his brothers are to form. Around Jesus, the shepherd who lays down his life out of love for his flock, brothers are assembled, as if around a hearth, certain of the Lord's presence, bonded together by him, and forever kept awake by the Gospel which is spirit and life. Based on this theological vision, Francis will enunciate the law that is meant to govern the relationships between men and women.

Let them love one another, as the Lord says: This is my commandment: Love one another as I have loved you (ER 11, 5; Jn 15, 12). And again: *Let us love our neighbor as ourselves. And if there is anyone who does not wish to love them as himself, at least let him do no harm to them, but rather do good* (2LtF 26, 27). And within the framework of a prayer: *and we may love our neighbor as ourselves by drawing them all to your love with our whole strength, by rejoicing over the good of others as over our own, by suffering with others at their misfortunes, and by giving offense to no one* (PrOF 5).

We must love the neighbor not only as oneself, but even more, as we have been loved by Jesus, with a love pushed to the final limits, the gift of one's own life.

But who are our neighbors? For Francis they are first of all those dear to him and whom, on many occasions, he refers to as *his blessed brothers* and whom he has led into the path of gospel perfection in the fraternity which he founded. To these he asks — and this is rare in religious literature — that they love one another with a love that is maternal. *Let each one love and care for his brother as a mother loves and cares for her son in those matters in which God has given him the grace* (ER 9, 11). He feels so strongly about this expression that he will keep it in the second, abridged, version of the Rule (LR 6, 8). This maternal love will find concrete expression according to the dictates of the situation: *Let each one confidently make known his need to another that the other might discover what is needed and minister to him* (ER 9, 10). This assumes that among brothers there exists the simple trust of a child towards his mother. We can say anything and demand everything from the other, assured that the other will receive it in as open a way as a mother towards her child. We must not, however, believe that Francis had an idyllic vision of fraternal relationships. He knows, and his Admonitions, among other texts, attest that we can suffer persecution from our brothers (Adm 3), that we can envy the good of another (Adm 8), that it is difficult to love those who strike us on the cheek (Adm 14), that we can require of others more than we are willing to give of ourselves (Adm 17), that it is heavy to bear the weaknesses of others (Adm 18) and to love those who seem to be only a useless burden (Adm 24).

The supreme love of one's neighbor is, as in the Gospel, the love of one's enemies, those who, in one way or another, offend us, wound us, or hurt us. In a key text of the second Rule (LR 10, 8–10) when Francis describes the work of the Spirit in those who possess it, after the prayer of a pure heart, he places, in an ascending scale of importance, the virtues of humility and patience concluding with love *for those who persecute, reprove and censure us, because the Lord says: Love your enemies, and pray for those who persecute and slander you* (Mt 5:44). The love of those who do not love us (and whom we do not love readily ...) is presented here as the highest spiritual attainment and that which renders us *perfect as the heavenly Father is perfect* (Mt 5:48), he who is kind towards *the ungrateful and the wicked* (Lk 6:35; ER 23, 8). Because such a love is impossible and because it is difficult to forgive, as an extension to this petition in the Our Father, one must repeat with Francis:

And what we do not completely forgive, make us Lord completely forgive, that we may truly love our enemies because of you and we may fervently intercede for them before you returning no one evil for evil (PrOF 8).

Moreover, this kindness and mercy cannot and must not limit itself to the narrow confines of the fraternity. A stunning text reminds the brothers: *Whoever comes to them, friend or foe, thief or robber, let him be received with kindness* (ER 7, 14). Whatever may be the historical circumstances of this strange recommendation, it affirms the unique value of every human being, even the most degraded. The primary attitude towards the stranger must be one of kindness: an affirming regard, a disposition to do good and to render service. And when we find ourselves in a hostile setting (in Francis' time the Muslim world and that of the crusades ...) we are required *not to engage in arguments or disputes but to be subject to every human creature for God's sake* (1 Pt 2:13; ER 16, 6). Such behavior, which goes counter to custom, provides a good demonstration of what Francis meant by the terms "brother" and "minor" (or lesser) in naming his fraternity. "Brother": someone trustworthy, convivial, kind; "minor": one who does not impose himself but who seeks to serve, who does not consider himself superior, but a servant.

A paradoxical text can serve as a conclusion to this meditation on the type of relationship that one must try to have with everyone. It serves as a conclusion to Francis' praise of three pairs of virtues: wisdom and simplicity, poverty and humility, charity and obedience. The last pair makes

one obey one's brother,
and be subject and submissive
to everyone in the world,
not only to people
but to every beast and
wild animal as well.

(Sa1V15–17)

This might strike us as a zen saying, or a call for a stoic, unreal, and out-of-touch approach to reality. Yet, in a way that is unexplainable, this prayer reaches us in our depths. For to love also means to obey, lend an ear and open one's heart to the other, make a place for them, renounce the pretense of going it alone, and stretch oneself to truly be with the other. In this sense, true love is submission (a reciprocal one ...) not only to all men and women, but also to the order in the world that one cannot modify (birth and death, events and history). What Francis means by the final clause: *but to every beast and wild animal as well* raises a question which leaves us in suspense, for one does not know how to do this or even how to respond. The answer to this question could be love: the type of love, mentioned previously in the Salutation, which *dissipates and confounds every carnal fear. For where there is love there is no fear* (Adm 27).

Reflection Questions

How do you find ways to ensure remembrance of God's loving presence in your life especially when you feel abandoned by God or lost? How far are you willing to go in your care and concern for others? Are you ready to give up your life so that others may live? Do you pray better alone, with two or three others or in a crowd? Where do you see yourself exercising power and control over others? Being subjected to the power and control/domination of others? Is reading the Gospel — words which are Spirit and Life — and trying to see how to put it into everyday practice part of your daily rhythm?

5
A Boundless Mercy

Focus Point

///////////////

God is all merciful; he forgives us and does not even remember our sins. In our everyday difficulties with others — especially those who hurt and wound us — our response must be to keep on forgiving and loving. These acts of mercy liberate us and others and make of us instruments of peace.

///////////////

To Brother N., minister: May the Lord bless you. I speak to you, as best I can, about the state of your soul. You must consider as grace all that impedes you from loving the Lord God and whoever has become an impediment to you, whether brothers or others, even if they lay hands on you. And may you want it to be this way and not otherwise.

> *And let this be for you the true obedience of the Lord God and my true obedience, for I know with certitude that it is true obedience. And love those who do those things to you and do not wish anything different from them, unless it is something the Lord God shall have given you. And love them in this and do not wish that they be better Christians. And let this be more than a hermitage for you.*
>
> *(LtMin)*

///////////

A man is assigned by Francis to serve a regional group of friars in their pursuit of the gospel life, hence his title of minister-servant. Who is he? What is his name (brother Elias perhaps)? No one knows. We do know that the difficulties of his task, caused no doubt by the mediocrity and the opposition of his brothers, have made him want to run away from them. He has withdrawn — or is about to do so — to a hermitage to find peace and to attend to the state of his soul. Francis addresses this simple, somewhat awkward text to him and it carries a stunning message. It contains a meditation on the boundless, tender mercy of God which this man must put into practice.

The text quoted at the head of this chapter asserts that the trials and difficulties encountered on the journey are to be considered as a grace. The journey at issue here is the gospel path in which one tries *to love the Lord God.* Nothing is greater or more exalting than a love enthusiastically turned toward God.

But in this case, the enthusiasm is cut short; something comes along that risks separating us from God. How are we to see our way through this impediment? Must we put it aside and try to get rid of it by running away? That is what the brother minister is thinking of doing and he acts on his thinking by isolating himself in a hermitage. He is pondering over *the state of his soul* convinced, no doubt, that the obstacles to love come from outside himself. Francis brusquely sets his thinking straight. In this case, the enemy, to be sure, is outside and he is clearly indicated: it is the neighbor: *some brothers or others.* Their behavior has nothing friendly about it. On the contrary, it even seems that their act of violence is more than mental or verbal, as is insinuated by the expression *even if they lay hands on you.* One would expect Francis to sympathize with the hermit and denounce the animosity of his associates which has pushed him to run away. But no, *you must consider all as grace.* Yes, the one (and those) who are an impediment to your love of the Lord God, consider them to be a grace for you.

As difficult as it is to accept a trial when it comes along and there is no way out, the only

correct attitude towards it is to submit to it with
a good heart: *may you want it to be this way and
not otherwise*. There is nothing fatalistic in all
this, but rather a certitude that such and such
a situation comes from God and one must welcome it by an act of obedience. The disciple
thus learns how to obey God's plan for him
and, Francis adds, my role is also to introduce
you to the mystery of God's will: *And let this be
for you the true obedience of the Lord God and my
true obedience, for I know with certitude that it is true
obedience*. The situations and the events which
impose themselves on us are also the voice of
the word of God. It serves no purpose to dream
of a world, a Church, or an ideal community
without faults; to accept the inevitable as real
— in this case difficulties caused by men who,
besides, are also dedicated to the Gospel — this
is the path of true obedience.

The reflection on the role of obstacles in the
spiritual life then focuses on the obstacle itself.
What prevents us from loving the Lord are not
impersonal situations, but beings of flesh and
blood: brothers. The minister in question has
fled from them; perhaps he is even tempted in his
heart to reject and to hate them, and he certainly
would have good reason to do so. What Francis
is beckoning for now becomes filled with pathos.
No, it is not hate but love that is called for: *love
those who do these things* (opposition, hostility,
blows?) *to you*. What one usually wishes for in

such a case is a change of heart, the conversion of one's enemies. We expect them to grow and to become better. Well, no! *Do not wish anything else from them, unless it is something the Lord God has given you.* If they have repented and reconciled themselves with you, all the better; if not, know how to wait and be patient. Allow time for them to grow (ultimately, counting above all on the Lord's work in them) and to progress according to their own rhythm.

But something even more surprising and which may even sound scandalous to our ears: *Do not wish that they be better Christians.* Nothing is more normal for a man of God than to wish with all one's soul that each one of his brothers be and become truly "Christians," united with Jesus Christ and gradually putting on more and more his image. Francis is as aware of this as any other believer. But he intuits in this wish, in the context which is that of the letter, the ambiguity that it can entail. I can ardently desire the conversion of my brother whose conduct wounds me and annoys me. In this way I will be at peace and he will no longer be an obstacle on my path. Such a desire, however, has something impure about it and this is what Francis denounces.

To enter into this perspective: submit to situations which we have no control over, love and bear patiently those that brought them on without expecting that things will change or improve immediately, *let this be more than a hermitage for*

you. Francis is favorable to life in a hermitage.
He even provided a rule to regulate how to live
in one and he himself frequently spent some
time in them; he does not denounce them as
such. But the flight of the minister to a hermitage to avoid the conflicts and the difficulties of
fraternal life seems to appear to him as an illu-
sionary search for a place and a world without
faults. The humble acceptance of everyday reality, the love which bears with others and is able
to forgive is better than life in a hermitage.

> *And if you have done this,*
> *I wish to know in this way if you love the*
> *   Lord and me,*
> *His servant and yours: that there is not any*
> *   brother in the world*
> *who has sinned — however much he could*
> *   have sinned —*
> *who, after he has looked into your eyes,*
> *   would ever*
> *depart without your mercy, if he is looking*
> *   for mercy.*
> *And if he were not looking for mercy,*
> *you would ask him if he wants mercy.*
> *And if he would sin a thousand times*
> *   before your eyes,*
> *love him more than me so that you may*
> *   draw him to the Lord;*
> *and always be merciful with brothers such*
> *   as these.*

And may you announce this to the guardians,
when you can that,
for your part, you are resolved to act in this
way.

(LtMin)

What follows in the letter deepens still further the inexhaustible mystery of mercy. The
minister was rebuked because of his flight and
firmly invited to love those who prevented him
from following through with his project such as
he had imagined it. Now, Francis, putting aside
for the moment the state of the minister's soul,
strikes his heart to draw from it the great well-
springs of mercy.

How is one to know if you love God and you
love me, his servant and also yours? There is a
great deal said about love in this initial phrase:
love of God, but also love of Francis. The man
in question felt himself impeded in his love of
God (and of Francis) and took flight. Now he
is summoned to manifest both loves, but in a
different manner. He will manifest it not by
running away but by opening wide his heart to
receive the sinful brother.

Two hypotheses are envisaged. The sinner
has recourse to his minister, as is, moreover,
called for by the Rule (LR 7, 1–2) and he *asks for*
mercy. What is at stake is no small matter: the
text assumes serious and multiple transgressions:
however much he could have sinned. The sinner

presents himself *to look into the eyes* of his brother. The two mentions of the eyes, here and a little later, catch our attention with this trait revealing in Francis a strong awareness of the human condition. Beyond mere words, necessary clarifications and even gestures, what counts is the face whose eyes serve as windows into the depths. Attention, compassion and kindness speak through the eyes louder than through words.

But it can happen that the sinner does not take the initiative of having recourse to the minister for mercy; he sticks obstinately to his evil ways; perhaps he even despairs of forgiveness. Then, it is up to me to go to him and to ask him, without imposing it, if he wants mercy. It is not said if, in such a case, it was accepted.

What follows is unheard of and leaves us breathless. Mercy, whether it is accepted or not, does not always have the effects anticipated. In the past the brother *has sinned however much he could have sinned*; once forgiven, it seems, nonetheless, that the brother has plunged headlong into evil: *he sins a thousand times before your eyes.* The minister's eyes, which were fountains of mercy, assist and are powerless before this overflow of sin. What must one do then, turn away from it and fall into despair? No, *love him more than me* (the minister loves Francis and the latter knows it ...). The only correct attitude in a situation which seems so desperate is to keep on loving, imitating God *whose favors are not exhausted nor his mercies spent but are renewed each morning* (Lam 3:22–23). For compassionate love — mercy — is stronger than whatever can adversely affect the body and the soul, no matter how seriously. This is why the minister is invited to love his unfortunate and unhappy brother more than Francis who is well spiritually.

This text is a hymn to mercy. By means of concrete language and events it expresses the central message of the Gospels: God loves the sinners and the sick and it is to save them that the Son has come into the world. Even where sins abound, grace can far surpass (Rm 5:20) and it is never permitted to despair of God's mercy.

Reflection Questions

Who are those whom you find most difficult to love or to forgive? Who are those whom you do not love as you should in your community or those you consider enemies? Can you extend your forgiveness to someone even if he or she does not ask for it? Can you accept others as they are, or are you constantly wishing that they correspond fully to your self-made image of perfection?

6
The Spiritual Journey

Focus Point

///////////////

The Trinity — Father, Son and Holy Spirit — is the source of our life and its final destination. The perfect communion that exists in God is a model and challenge for all our relationships. In order to realize in ourselves this life of self-donation and mutual fulfillment we must accept our own powerlessness in using our own efforts to do so. It is a gift of the Holy Spirit that cleanses, enlightens and inflames us allowing us to follow the footsteps of Jesus, the beloved of the Father, and make our way to the discovery of the Father as the ultimate realization and mystery of our lives.

///////////////

Almighty, eternal, just and merciful God,
give us miserable ones
the grace to do for You alone

what we know you want us to do
and always to desire what pleases You.
Inwardly cleansed,
interiorly enlightened
and inflamed by the fire of the Holy Spirit,
may we be able to follow
in the footprints of Your beloved Son,
our Lord Jesus Christ,
and, by Your grace alone,
may we make our way to You,
Most High,
Who live and rule
in perfect Trinity and simple Unity,
and are glorified
God almighty,
forever and ever.
Amen

(LtOrd 50–52)

//////////

*D*uring the final years of his life (ca. 1224), Francis reviews the various experiences that he has lived and which have taught him how broad and long the spiritual journey can be. Rather than speak of it in a theoretical manner, he will describe it by using the framework of a prayer with a liturgical style and structure. This prayer comes at the end of a long letter addressed, because of his sickness, to all the brothers.

The various names given to God express his greatness: *almighty*, *most high*, *eternal*, and his relationship to humankind: *just*, *merciful*. The approach to God is never neutral: his mystery reveals itself to human beings initially in its otherness, one which is beyond all experience because of its inaccessible heights, its majestic power, and its duration, which is eternal. Together with this transcendent dimension, which for Francis is always foremost, God's relationship to humankind is revealed. He is a God who sees the depths of the person, can discern and weigh the good and the evil because he is *just*. And when his gaze discovers the fragility, the powerlessness, and the misery which characterize the human condition, it is his emotional side, his brokenheartedness and his *mercy* which discloses itself. This twofold face of the divine mystery, far from keeping Francis at a distance, pushes him to move forward in his exploration of the unfathomable riches of God. For him, God is not a being who is immobile and static; there are certain realities with which he is pleased and which he wants; towards humankind God is generous, a giver. This is why Francis can speak of *what pleases* God, *what he wants* and, as someone needy, in the name of all humankind, address himself to him, and say: *grant us*. To complete Francis' language on God, we must also take note of the three expressions near the end of the text: *You who live and rule and are glorified.* God is boundless life, a "perpetual fountain of unpredictable newness"; he rules, not as despot, but as a joyful "choreographer of immortality"; and he bursts forth with glorious splendor.

The One to whom the prayer is addressed is not a God closed in on himself but rather the God of revelation: *the Father of the beloved Son, our Lord Jesus Christ.* The Holy Spirit is also mentioned. Thus it is the total mystery of the living God, highlighted in a text which is nonetheless brief. Moreover, two expressions taken from the liturgy underline this total mystery of God: *perfect Trinity and simple Unity.* We could see in these expressions simply a repetition of stereotyped formulas. But if we try to penetrate their meaning, one which Francis certainly noticed — each time in his writings the word *Trinity* is accompanied by its contrary, *Unity* — *we* are struck by the depths of his theological intuition. *Perfect Trinity* represents an affirmation of God's otherness, the real difference which exists between each of the persons within the divine communion. Each person is distinct, other, and perfectly accepted and respected as such. But this distinctiveness of each person is also situated within the dimension of *simple Unity*. Diversity and autonomy, far from bursting asunder the relationship and creating distance or division between the divine persons, flow back into the One. Otherness and Unity, which are always in impossible tension among humans, weld into marvelous harmony in the Triune God. The otherness and the same-ness neither exclude nor neutralize one another. Thus, the mystery of the Trinity is a model and a challenge for every human relationship.

In contrast with this sumptuous and overflow-ing plenitude of the divine life we are presented with the feebleness of the human being desig-nated by only one word: *miserable,* or needy. One might say that this word, concerning the misery or the unhappiness of the human condition, is there to draw down God's mercy — his custom-ary behavior towards human beings — closer to us. For if we, human beings, are *miserable,* which Francis will repeat often, we are nonetheless capable, with God's help, *for Himself and by His grace alone,* of accomplishing a great deal. We can know what God wants and discover, in our lives and in the message addressed to us, God's plan for us. We can, likewise, want with a heartfelt desire, and by efficacious choices, what pleases God, much like Jesus who "always does what pleases his Father" (Jn 8:29). We can above all *do,* concretely put into action, after having dis-covered its implications, the will of God. Even more, after having abandoned ourselves to the work of the Spirit in us, we are able, to *follow in the footprints of Christ,* and *make our way* to the supreme goal, the encounter with the Father in God's Trinitarian mystery, one filled with life and glory. Once again, we, the *miserable ones,* are not condemned to wallow in our misery. God calls us to a high destiny, traces the path to it for us and gives us, in order to move forward, the necessary dynamism to do so.

In human behavior, Francis distinguishes two dimensions: active and passive. He assumes that we already know, or at least are capable of knowing, what the will of God consists of; that it is within our power to be filled with wonder over what pleases God and, above all, to put into action what does so. But this is not enough. Other demands impose themselves which human effort alone cannot accomplish. We will need to pass through a path where the initiative does not come from us but from the Holy Spirit. It is this passive dimension which the following lines describe:

> *Inwardly purified*
> *interiorly enlightened*
> *and inflamed by the fire of the Holy Spirit....*

We have turned ourselves towards God, asking him for the grace to begin our journey and to realize God's plan of love for us. Suddenly we become aware that it is an undertaking that lies beyond our capacity to choose and commit ourselves to, and that what is needed is an intervention which comes from outside ourselves. This other dimension consists in the Spirit of the Father and the Son, the holy breath of God, which is also a fire which turns into a conflagration. The Spirit alone is capable of putting the heart through a mysterious alchemical process, cleansing its inner depths of all impurities, irradiating it with its dazzling light, and above all setting it ablaze by its fire. This triple transformation (the three ways of the spiritual tradition: purification, illumination, union) Francis attributes directly to the work of the Holy Spirit, a fire which purifies, enlightens, and burns with love. Human effort fades into the background and yields to a divine energy which alone can accomplish what no human being can: be inflamed by love.

Little by little we begin to see more clearly what the rather vague expression, *do what we know you want us to do*, means. What the Father wants is to see human beings invested with his Spirit, handed over to his mysterious operation which will make them clean, clear-sighted and stricken by love. Only then can we move forward in the footprints of his Beloved Son. To follow in the traces set by Christ, as asked for in the first letter of Peter (2:21) which Francis will quote on a number of occasions, does not mean primarily to redo the gestures of the human life of Jesus as if we were always living in his company, but to enter into the total meaning of the mystery of his life, death and glory. It means to relive the *blessed passion* of the Lord, accept, in humility and inner poverty, the contradictions and the sufferings of life in fidelity to the Gospel and its promises.

However, to walk in the footsteps of Christ, which is at the center of the prayer, is not the ultimate goal; it is but a stage in the process. That towards which everything converges is expressed by the phrase:

to make our way to You.

The end of the journey consists in the encounter of men and women with God. We walk in the manner of the Son and with him, having in our hearts the fire of the Paraclete who pursues its work in us. Finally, one day — but when? — we will arrive at our destination. The summit will have been reached where awaits us the One for whom we have been made and whom everything in us has never ceased, even if by many wayward turns, to seek and to desire. He is the Father towards whom the Spirit was moving us and to whom the Son led us, and uniquely the Most High, yet never solitary, for a plurality (Trinity) and a unity at the same time. We make our way to this encounter with God not to assist at a spectacle, but to share, as a friend and as a partner, the life, the reign, and the glory of the One who gives himself to us, after having drawn us to him. This intimacy beyond telling, however, does not, for Francis, entail too close a familiarity: God remains eternally the *Most High* (in relationship to humans) and the *all-powerful.*

All these astonishing considerations are contained in a text consisting of only one sentence and presenting itself as a prayer. This text is also noteworthy because of its insistence on persistent supplication. To make known our requests so that they may be heard, even if the misery of the human condition is mentioned, it is nonetheless who God is in himself that we call upon: *for You alone.* It is because God is God, because in the depths of his being he is not centered upon himself but open and turned towards men and women, that, in support of each of our supplications, we can rely on these depths, make an appeal to this abyss, the passionate love which God has for men and women.

At the same time that Francis makes strong demands upon us and thus deems that we can respond to them, he knows, along with St. Paul and the entire Christian tradition, that everything comes from God and depends upon him. If he does not say that we are saved by faith alone, he will say, and this is no doubt more radical: *by Your grace alone* as in this text, or elsewhere: *by your mercy alone* (ER 23, 8). To be sure, to be swept along in the waters of kindness and tenderness (grace and mercy) we must throw ourselves in its streams which never cease to well up from their source at the very heart of the Trinity for the life of the world.

Reflection Questions

Do you have an awareness of the role of each person of the Trinity in your life? Reflect upon some moments in which you have acknowledged your powerlessness and experienced God's grace in your life. Do you start your day with the firm desire to do God's will come what may? Do you trust that God will grant you the graces that you need in all the circumstances of your life? Given that the Trinity is a mystery of self-donation and communion, how does this contrast with the individualist culture in which we live?

7
The Pure Heart

Focus Point

///////////////

To live a free life means to grow in our capacity to live without property (*sine proprio*) whether spiritual or material. It is with such a purified heart that we are able to perceive God's activity in every facet of our lives and our world and to fall on our knees in adoration.

///////////////

> *Blessed are the pure of heart for they shall*
>   *see God.*
> *The truly pure of heart are those who gaze*
>   *from*
> *above at earthly realities, seek heavenly*
>   *ones, and*
> *never cease adoring and seeing the Lord God*
> *living and true with a pure heart and spirit.*
>
>   *(Adm 16)*

///////////////

*H*ow? What steps need to be taken? What type of gaze or intuition is called for to have access to an experiential knowledge of God? It is to such a question that Francis wants to respond by commenting on the Beatitude of the pure of heart.

That by which human beings approach God is not the eye, but the *heart*, which in Francis' biblical vocabulary designates the unifying center, the ultimate depths, that which constitutes and moves the person. According to his custom, Francis combines the word *heart* — by itself a blind energy — with another word, *spirit*, which means the light of knowledge, "the heart's way of knowing." It is then only the heart, enlightened by knowledge, which can encounter God.

And this heart must be *pure*. The initial and spontaneous interpretation of this term would be: without blemish or any impurities. Aside from the fact that this is an impossible demand to realize in this life — what indeed does a heart without blemish consist of? — and which could, by this fact, push us to a state of despair; this is not the biblical meaning which Francis gives to the word pure. As the explanation provided by the text of the Admonition indicates, the pure heart is a heart freed from superficiality and centered on what matters and what is true. Thus the pure heart can:

gaze from above at earthly realities,
seek heavenly ones, and
never cease adoring and seeing God.

For Francis, this implies a certain attitude towards reality. The latter is seen in its twofold component: *earthly* — immediate, perceptible — and *celestial,* that which is other, "from above," and in itself inaccessible to the senses. What is *earthly,* the empirical and pragmatic side of things, will be looked at differently, from above, from afar. To see earthly realities otherwise means to perceive both their relativity — in order not to put our whole heart into them — and their opening to a beyond, the depth dimension of everything that is. The *celestial* is precisely the mystery dimension present in everything and whose absolute center is God himself. If we must look from above, as a passerby, and with a gaze directed at what is deepest in the reality immediately before us, it requires that we seek, be ever on the alert, be in a permanent search for what allows itself to be glimpsed in the depths or over and above everything, *the Lord God.* Who is not an inanimate idea or a false idol but the Lord *living and true.*

Contact with the mystery of the living and true God — through earthly realities seen otherwise and by an unceasing quest for the heavenly realities — is accomplished through adoration and vision: *they never cease adoring and seeing.*

What is primary is not vision (the eye) but adoration which is a matter of the heart. *To adore*
connotes a movement of stupefaction, a state
of awe, the need for inner and outer prostration
which takes hold of human beings when they
approach the inaccessible mystery. This adoration of the heart, however, is accompanied by
seeing, a word which in the Johannine language
familiar to Francis designates faith and experiential awareness.

This brief commentary of the Beatitude
presents, in a condensed description, the basic
structure of the discovery of and the approach
to God. A heart which, unified and centered,
seeks and pursues throughout all of created
reality, earthly as well as celestial, that which
is the only object of its desire, its adoration
and its vision: the living God. This is what a
pure heart means for Francis. Not an unsul-
lied heart, but a heart which has taken leave
of its virtues and its sins, which has gone out
of itself to search for the One who is present
everywhere and nowhere.

After this somewhat schematic description
of the journey of a pure heart, let us meditate
on a passionate exhortation in which Francis,
addressing himself to his brothers — and
beyond these to all men and women — begs
them not to forget the essential: *to have one's
heart turned towards God.*

Therefore, let us all be very much on our
    guard
that under the guise of some reward or
    assistance,
we do not lose or take our mind away from
    God.
But, in the holy love that is God I beg all ...
after overcoming every impediment
and putting aside every care and anxiety,
to serve, love, honor, and adore the Lord God
with a pure heart and pure mind
in whatever way they are able to do so
for that is what he wants above all else.
And let us always make a home and a
    dwelling-place there
for Him who is the Lord God almighty,
Father, Son and Holy Spirit....

                              (ER 22, 25–27)

We can only adore and see God with a desiring, and by that factor, a pure heart. But this does not happen by itself. Tangled in a network of toils and troubles, held back and scattered by them, we can forget the ultimate concern which aims for the experience of God and from that experience a different perception of the world.

We must not *lose* sight of this opening, the wounded heart, and turn elsewhere and away from the only One who can heal it. Many things need to be done which in themselves are just and even necessary. It is normal to earn one's living (a salary), and to do this one has to *work*; *assistance* to others also imposes itself either as part of one's duty or for the sake of charity. But we must not, *under the guise* of these inevitable and indispensable occupations, turn our hearts away from God. One must perform these activities because they are part of living, but we must perform them in such a way that the ultimate concern does not become secondary and get snuffed out. To be sure, a perfect balance is never a given nor ever definitely attained. Human occupations in all their diversity take up the greater portion of life and require application, attention, and competence. The effort and the concentration that is needed, however, can take hold of the depths of our hearts and render them inattentive to *what God wants above all else.* The solution, however, is not to be found in the suppression or the reduction of our current activities, but in the manner in which they are managed.

It is in the name of what is greatest and most sacred, *in the holy love which is God*, that Francis implores us to *overcome every impediment and put aside every care and anxiety*, in a word, not to allow ourselves to be seduced or fascinated by diversions. In order to do this, no concrete means are indicated or suggested. No doubt, in Francis' eyes, these means consist in not fleeing obstacles, but in concentrating on the goal to be attained. This goal consists in *serving, loving, honoring and adoring the Lord God in whatever way we are best able to do so.* No particular prescription is given and a large space is left open for personal initiative and discernment: each one must discover *the best way to do so* according to one's experience, strength and life rhythm. The goal to be pursued is characterized by four words which follow one another in an order which is perhaps not fortuitous: *serve, love, honor and adore.* The *service* called for is the concrete realization of the demands of the Gospel towards God and human beings, fidelity to the commandments in the concreteness of human existence. *To love* consists in a receptivity to the moving and overwhelming love of God for us and our feeble attempts to reciprocate that love. The next two words, which form a pair, *to honor and adore,* belong in the same category: before the mystery of God, men and women, even if smitten by love, can only stand before it with an attitude of sovereign respect and fearful adoration. This movement of our entire being — a pure heart and spirit — is what God wants *above all else.* Men and women, however, are not the only ones searching. God is also a being of desire which makes him turn his gaze towards us. More than anything else, beyond his autonomy and beatitude, God seeks to become our companion.

It is precisely this incredible intimacy between human beings and God which introduces us to the final passage of the text. It combines an allusion to the Gospel of John (14:22), "we will come to him and make our dwelling place with him," with another text drawn from the letter to the Ephesians (2:22), "to become a dwelling place for God in the Spirit." All the steps described so far: freedom from cares, efforts to serve, love and adore, the centering and purifying of the heart and the spirit, culminate in the secret coming of the Father, the Son and the Spirit in the pure heart. The latter thus becomes a home, a dwelling place. Inhabitation, mutual indwelling — "as you, Father, are in me, and I in you, that they too be in us" (Jn 17:21) — suggests a type of union which surpasses the conjugal one wherein juxtaposition subsists. To be in one another, without losing otherness, is the supreme dream of every love. What is realized in ineffable plenitude in the Trinitarian communion is offered as a gratuitous gift to the one who, with a pure heart, *does not cease adoring and seeing the Lord God living and true.*

Reflection Questions

What type of gaze or intuition is called for to have access to an experiential knowledge of God? What are the priorities of your life? What other desires compete with your desire for God? How do your worries or anxieties become an obstacle to experiencing God and living fully each day? What is the place of adoration in your life?

8
What the Pure Heart Sees

Focus Point

////////////

Thanksgiving is a sign of true and liberated consciousness. To be able to be thankful for all that happens to us and in the world opens us up to God's merciful love and compassion. It is at the Eucharist that this movement of thanksgiving finds its greatest and most fitting expression. It is also at the Eucharist that our lives are blessed, broken and handed over for others and the world.

////////////

All-powerful, most holy,
Almighty and supreme God,
*   Holy and just Father,*
Lord King of heaven and earth
we thank you for Yourself

for through Your holy will
and through Your only Son
with the Holy Spirit
You have created all things spiritual and
  corporal
and, after making us in your image and
  likeness,
You placed us in paradise.
Through our own fault we fell.

We thank you
for as through your Son You created us,
so through your holy love
with which You loved us
You brought about His birth as true God
  and true man
by the glorious, ever virgin, most blessed,
  holy Mary
and You willed to redeem us captives,
through His cross and blood and death.

We thank You
for Your Son Himself will come again
in the glory of His majesty
to send into the everlasting fire
the wicked ones
who have not done penance
and have not known You
and to say to all those
who have known You, adored You and
  served You in penance:

"Come, you, blessed of my Father,
receive the kingdom prepared for you
from the beginning of the world."

(ER, 23, 1-4)

////////////

*W*hile this admirable hymn of thanksgiving, which Francis places at the
conclusion of the first Rule, sings lyrically of
the mystery of the Trinitarian communion, it
does not, all the same, separate this mystery
from its works which unfold in history. What
the pure heart sees, obviously foremost, is the
magnificence of the *holy Father with his beloved
Son and the Holy Spirit,* the Paraclete, but also,
and inseparately, the human person as the *image
and likeness of God,* as well as *all things spiritual
and corporal.* The object of the spiritual vision
consists in the totality of reality with its basis
and center: the Triune God, the fount of all that
is and, *through the holy love,* the unfolding of the
human adventure.

The contemplation of the mystery with the
almighty Father as the focus also broadens to
include the Trinitarian communion with an
emphasis on the role of the Son, and then considers the totality of the divine work of salvation, its *economy.*

The figure of the Father is enthroned at the
center of the text. His greatness is suggested

by the accumulation of names and attributes (9 in all!) which all relate to his transcendence. He is powerful, separate, totally other, elevated on high, master of the universe: God! Only his name, Father — *holy and just*, as he is called by Jesus in John's Gospel (17:11, 25) — brings him near to us.

The thanksgiving, which is repeated three times, is directed first of all to the Father by means of a dense and mysterious expression: *we thank You for Yourself*, for who You are. We are to give thanks to God *for His immense glory*, independently of his works, simply because God is God. All the more so because the divine inner life is not closed in on itself: *the holy will* of the Father, his plan based on *the holy love with which He loved us,* makes him spring forth from himself and shape *with His two hands* — his only Son and the Holy Spirit — the universe, human beings and human history. The deepest center of God, his "himself," is perceived as already turned towards human beings; his will and his love are aquiver with a *holy* impatience to establish a relationship with us.

The Father, who is the recipient of adoration and thanksgiving, never appears without the Son. The deeds of the *only Son*, the beloved, as Isaac for Abraham; his role in the creative work, his birth in the flesh, his identity as *true God and true man*, his redemptive passion: *cross, blood and death*, as well as his final coming *in the glory of*

His majesty — all are clearly designated. If it is the Father who acts, he always puts his Son at the forefront.

The Spirit appears only once in the text and as a divine force intervening alongside the Son in the work of creation.

As far as human beings are concerned, they are present in every line of the poem: they are the *we* who sing the song of thanksgiving. In truth, everything is centered on human beings as much as on God. They are considered as the crowning point of the creation of *all things corporal and spiritual*. As glorious image and likeness of the Trinity, they are made for the happiness of paradise. Their fault, which has rendered them slaves to sin and death, aroused *the holy love* of the Father and moved him to send his own Son into the world for our liberation. Because of this fact, human beings have a dramatic decision to make: either *know, love, and serve God* by a radical change of life (*penance*), or refuse to do so and pay the unhappy consequences. For those who have not been receptive to *the holy love*, did not acknowledge it and did not want to change their lives, exclude themselves from salvation. The fire of love, rather than setting them ablaze, will devour them. But those who lent themselves to this love will attain the place of happiness which awaits them since the beginning of the world, where, *blessed by the Father*, they will eternally reign with him.

The cosmic dimension is also present in this fresco. Even before the creation of human beings, *all things spiritual*, as a work of love, are presented: the invisible world, especially the angelic one, which Francis often mentions in his writings, and material realities, *all things corporal.*

The vision which Francis presents is not a static one: it encompasses the movement of history from its origins in paradise to the end of time. This history consists of three stages: the creation and the fall of human beings; the birth of the Son and his salvific death; finally, the glorious parousia and the return to paradise, the *kingdom prepared from the beginning of the world.* Noteworthy is the special place reserved for *the glorious, ever-virgin, most blessed, holy Mary*; four qualifying terms are attributed to her.

What Francis perceives with his heart and his spirit does not lead him to compose an abstract exposition of his vision. It is within the framework of a lyrical, Eucharistic and doxological hymn that he celebrates the marvelous plan of the Father being realized in the world. The grandiose vision of the Triune God involved in a love struggle with human beings stirs up wonderment and thanksgiving in Francis. What he contemplates, the unfolding of the plan *of the holy will and the holy love*, is beautiful and harmonious. It is living theater with various actors and contrasting destinies: Father-Son-Paraclete, the Virgin Mary, and human beings as images of God. Before such marvels what can human beings do if not *be thankful*: acknowledge the kindness and the splendor which is manifested and extol its gratuitous liberality with full voice.

This text, whose central themes have just been highlighted, can rightly be considered as a paradigm of contemplation as Francis understood it. It responds to the question of what the pure heart sees when it encounters the mystery of God. And the response is: the pure heart sees everything but in a different manner. It sees everything: it sees the heavenly Father celebrated because of who he is and acting in history with his Son and the Holy Spirit; it sees the *world pregnant with God filling all to overflowing* (Angela of Foligno); it sees human beings both in their excellence and in their misery, from which God saves them; it sees *the visible and invisible universe;* it sees the movement of *the holy love* of God in the vicissitudes of history. Thus *to contemplate,* for Francis, means to have a total vision, a "holistic one," made hierarchical and balanced, of what is truly real.

The wonder stirred by such a vision wells up into a boundless act of thanksgiving which human beings by themselves cannot fully perform so they must hand it over to the care of the Son and the Holy Spirit. Thus it is an epiclesis which ends the Eucharist sung by Francis:

Because all of us, wretches and sinners,
are not worthy to pronounce Your name,
we humbly ask
our Lord Jesus Christ,
Your beloved Son,
in whom You are well pleased,
together with the Holy Spirit,
the Paraclete,
to give You thanks,
for everything
as it pleases You and Him,
who always satisfies You in everything,
through whom You have done so much for us.
Alleluia!

(ER 23)

Reflection Questions

What are the gifts you have received for which you are most thankful? What are those you tend to neglect to be thankful for? In your daily relationships, do you express your gratitude for the gifts of others in your life, who they are for you and how they provide for your happiness and well-being? Do you find time to thank God for and in the wondrous mystery of Father, Son and Holy Spirit? Do you look forward to the return of Jesus in his glory?

9
The Word of the Father

Focus Point

When the disciples wanted to discover the secret of Jesus' intimacy with the Father and learn how to pray, Jesus taught them what has become known to us as *The Lord's Prayer.* It is the most perfect of all prayers and contains all that is needed for growing in our relationship with God and with others. It offers a perfect balance between the opening petitions addressed to God and those that follow addressing the needs of humanity. When it is said with attentiveness, it can be assured that something graceful will happen in our lives and in our world. When proclaimed in the context of the Eucharist, it prepares us to receive the body and blood of Christ most worthily and beneficially.

Give us this day:
in remembrance, understanding, and
  reverence
of that love which our Lord Jesus Christ
  had for us
and of those things that He said and did
  and suffered for us,
our daily bread:
Your own beloved Son, our Lord Jesus
  Christ.

(PrOF 1, 6)

//////////////

When he comments on the prayer of the Lord, the *Our Father*, Francis gives a directly Christological meaning to the petition for daily bread. The daily bread, without which human beings cannot live, is *the beloved Son, our Lord Jesus Christ.* For the life of the believer to have a meaning, for it to blossom and last, he or she must encounter Jesus Christ. What Francis sees, first of all, in the mystery of Jesus, is *the love He has for us.* To eat this bread which is Jesus is to fully receive in our hearts the overwhelming revelation of his excessive love for all human beings. The expression *for us* that we find in key parts of the Creed — "*for us* and for our salvation he came down from heaven; crucified *for us* under Pontius Pilate" — is repeated twice in Francis' brief text. It expresses the certitude and deep emotion which human beings experience before this incomprehensible love. This love of Jesus has manifested itself in his words, his deeds, and in the sufferings he endured: *what He said and did and suffered.* The burning center of the mystery of Jesus is his love as attested by his teachings, his works and his passion.

To eat this bread means to receive and to *remember* who Jesus was, to attempt to penetrate, in remembrance, the unfathomable riches of His life through an effort of understanding and by means of an act of adoration filled with *reverence.* Once again Francis condenses, in a brief and simple phrase, a complete method for the contemplation of the person of Jesus: to remember, understand, adore, not outer aspects, but the heart of everything: *the love He has for us.*

In another passage, which serves as an opening for his exposition of Christian life in the world, Francis provides a more ample vision of the mystery of the Word made flesh.

> *The most high Father made known from heaven*
> *through His holy angel Gabriel this Word of the Father*
> *— so worthy, so holy and glorious —*
> *in the womb of the holy and glorious Virgin Mary,*
> *from whose womb He received the flesh of our humanity and frailty.*

Though He was rich,
He wished, together with the most Blessed
*   Virgin, His mother,*
to choose poverty in the world beyond all else.

And as His Passion was near,
He celebrated the Passover with His disciples
and, taking bread, gave thanks, blessed and
*   broke it, saying:*
Take and eat: This is my body.
And taking the cup He said:
This is My blood of the new covenant
which will be poured for you and for many
for the forgiveness of sins.
Then He prayed to his Father, saying:
Father, if it can be done, let this cup pass
*   from me.*
And His sweat became as drops of blood
falling on the ground.
Nevertheless, he placed His will in the will
*   of His Father,*
saying: Father, let Your will be done;
not as I will, but as You will.
His Father's will was such
that His blessed and glorious Son,
whom He gave to us and who was born for us,
should offer Himself through His own blood
as a sacrifice and oblation on the altar of
*   the cross:*
not for Himself through Whom all things
*   were made,*

> *but for our sins, leaving us an example*
> *that we might follow His footprints.*
>
> > *(1LtF 4–13)*

Let us admire the theological balance of this fresco, its correctness as well as its lyricism.

Everything is focused on the Son, but this Son is, here again, inseparable from the Father, always in his presence and pursuing a painful but trusting dialogue with him. Of this Father, he is the Word, *worthy, holy, glorious,* which awakens in us a sentiment of admiration and respect. He *is rich beyond all things* (2 Cor 8:9) by reason of the fullness of the divine being which he possesses with the Father and the Spirit, *and because everything was made by Him.* Francis, in harmony with the faith of the Church professed in the Creed, considers the mystery of Christ from above and then in a descending fashion. In fact, it is the most high Father who, from heaven, sends his powerful Word so that it takes on, in silence, *the true flesh of our humanity and frailty.* It is not because of its value and dignity but because of its limits and frailty — suffering and death — that the true flesh of humanity is evoked here.

The descent from the heights of glory to the frailty of the flesh announced by a messenger, the angel Gabriel, finds its fulfillment *in the womb of the holy and glorious Virgin Mary.* She is, nonetheless, the one who will give to the Word, so worthy of the Father, the flesh with its share of suffering and death. Even more, she will be the accomplice and the companion of his Son in the choice of poverty. Poverty of material goods, no doubt, but above all the obscurity, the hiddenness, and the humility of the One "who annihilated himself taking on the condition of a servant" (Ph 2:7). The sentence "he came down from heaven and ... took on the flesh of the Virgin Mary" is dramatized by Francis. He accentuates the contrast between the heights of the glory and the frailty of the flesh. From the coming in the flesh, Francis, circumventing the earthly life of Jesus, goes directly not to the Passion itself but to the *Passover which Jesus celebrated with his disciples.* In the manner of a liturgist, he solemnly redoes the narrative of the institution of the Eucharist. The Eucharist, as a living memorial of the death-resurrection of the Lord *who cannot die again because he is eternally victorious and glorious* (LtOrd 22), occupies an important place in his vision. It is through it, ritual and sacrament, that *the Lord is always with His faithful as he Himself says: Behold, I am with you until the end of time* (Adm 1, 22). What he said, did, and suffered for us is made present in the paschal event of the Crucified-Risen One.

The deep reality of the Eucharist, beyond the presence of the body and the blood, is, according to Francis, the trusting handing over of the Son into the steady hands of the Father. Troubled by the perspective of his destiny — passion and death to the point of sweating drops of blood — the Son wishes to be delivered from it while at the same time abandoning himself totally to the will of the Father. When he speaks of the Son handing himself over to the will of the Father, Francis uses terms of endearment and calls him *blessed and glorious.* This Son has been given to us and has been born for us — an allusion to the Isaiah text proclaimed at Christmas (Is 9:5) that Francis uses in the Psalm for this feast (Ps 15:7). The blessed Son, the child given to us and received, will be, like and even more so than Isaac, offered in sacrifice. Different from Isaac (Gn 22:16), for he is asked to offer himself freely with his own blood as a liturgical sacrifice on the cross. It is not the hand of the Father which will immolate him; as priest he is his own victim. What does this sacrificial language mean: to offer oneself, blood, sacrifice, victim, altar? Borrowed from the Old Testament and also from the Letter to the Hebrews, these images evoke the total gift, the sacrifice made out of love for humankind. The love of the Father who has not spared his own Son but handed him over to us (Rm 8:32), the love of the Son who sacrifices himself, not for the Father but for, or rather, *because of our sins.*

We are surprised not to see any mention of the Resurrection in this unfolding of the paschal event of Christ. It is not that Francis is unaware of it or is silent about it. In the Psalm which

he composed for the Office of None on Good
Friday — the hour of Christ's death — after a
detailed description of the sufferings and the
descent *into the dust of death*, he puts this trium-
phal song in the mouth of the Crucified:

> *I have slept and risen*
> *and my most holy Father has received me*
>   *with glory.*
> *Holy Father, You held my right hand*
> *led me with your counsel*
> *and have taken me up with glory…*
> *… See, see that I am God, says the Lord.*
> *I shall be exalted among the nations*
> *and exalted on the earth…*
> *… And we know, that He is coming*
> *that He will come to judge the earth.*

(OfP)

Thus, for Francis, inspired by John's Gospel
(Jn 8:28; 12:32), the elevation of Jesus on the
Cross is, at the same time, his rising into glory,
a manifestation of his universal lordship, and a
proclamation of his return. Francis' vision of
Christ includes every important element of the
mystery.

The final sentence speaks of *the example
that Jesus has left us so that we may follow his footprints.* This passage, taken from the first Letter
of Peter (2:21), occupies an important place in
Francis' spirituality. He quotes it five times in
his writings. It does not entail, as the context

indicates, reproducing the facts and deeds of Jesus' earthly life, but to borrow from and take part in his entire itinerary: from the bosom of the Father until his return in glory. To enter into the mystery of the humiliation and the poverty of the Word *leaving the royal throne to come down into the Virgin's womb* (Adm 1, 16); to drink the Eucharistic cup in which glimmers *the blood of incorruptible love* (Ignatius of Antioch); to hand over, in every situation and in every event, *one's will in the will of the Father*, and if necessary to the point of death; to enter, after the sufferings of the passion, into the glory wherein the Father uplifts His Son, *to be there where He is and to see his glory* (Jn 17:24; ER 22, 55) — this is, indeed, what it means to *follow in the footprints of Christ.*

It is to such contemplation that we are led to by the *remembrance, understanding and reverence of the love that Jesus Christ had for us and what He said for us, and did, and suffered.*

Reflection Questions

To which petition of the Lord's Prayer do you most relate? Why is it important that God's will be done and not yours? Do you see a connection between the daily bread element and starving in the world and the increasing gap between the rich and the poor? How does receiving the Eucharist help you remember what Jesus did and how he suffered for us on the cross and was risen from the dead?

10
The Glorious Lady and the Saints

Focus Point

As a poor woman living at the margins of the dominant culture of her time and awaiting in eager expectation the coming of the Messiah, the great liberator of her people, Mary received in the astounding message of the angel the annunciation that she was blessed among women and would be the God-bearer of the Promised One. Because of her "yes" to this message a Savior was born who *would cast down the mighty from their thrones, fill the hungry with good things, send the rich away empty* (Magnificat).

Hail, O Lady,
Holy Queen,
Mary, holy Mother of God,

Who are the Virgin made Church,
   chosen by the most holy Father in heaven
whom He consecrated with His most holy
   beloved Son
and with the Holy Spirit the Paraclete,
in whom there was and is
all fullness of grace and every good.

Hail His Palace!
Hail His Tabernacle!
Hail His Dwelling!
Hail His Robe!
Hail His Handmaid!
Hail His Mother!

(SalBVM)

//////////////

*E*ach time that Francis contemplates the mystery of God in its totality and God's works in the world — as in the two preceding meditations — the figure of the Virgin Mary appears. She is as a watershed which marks the before and the after, the doorway through which salvation makes its way into the world. Her name is enshrined by numerous qualifiers which high-light her dignity: she is *glorious, ever-virgin, most blessed, holy* (ER 23, 3: 2LtF, 4, 5). Other than her role in salvation — Francis cannot speak of sal-vation without mentioning Mary's important role in it — two beautiful texts are explicitly dedicated to her. The first is a song filled with wonder and praise called *A Salutation of the Blessed Virgin Mary*. No petition, no praise and no acts of thanksgiving are formulated; only a pure and disinterested gaze lovingly centered on the object of its contemplation.

The first sentence begins with the Latin word *Ave* (translated by *hail*), and is followed by a string of four names: *lady, queen, virgin, mother* which the adjective *holy* qualifies. It is with great respect and with great courtesy that Francis addresses himself to Mary as Lady and Queen. She is no ordinary woman but *the holy mother of God* (*Genitrix*, the translation of the Greek, *Theotokos*), from which comes her incomparable dignity. He sees her as a virgin in majesty as in Romanesque sculptures. Mother, she is also *Virgin made Church*. Mary appears to Francis as a prefiguration, an image, and an icon of the Church; what she is now, the Church is called to become.

The word "Church" has a double meaning: the community of the faithful and the material structure in which this community assembles (*house of the Church*, as an old tradition puts it). In our text the twofold meanings superimpose themselves. Like the people of God and Abraham and Sarah, her ancestors in the faith, Mary is the chosen one; she is the one selected by *the most holy Father in heaven* who is the source of all initiatives because he is the fount

and beginning of all that is. From Mary's election we move to her consecration. The image of
the Church as the people of God dovetails into
that of the Church as a material structure. The
structure is consecrated with great solemnity:
*the Father, the most beloved Son and the Holy Spirit
Paraclete* concelebrate this dedication. The rea-
soning behind this election and this consecration is very understandable: the Church which
is identified with the Virgin Mary provides the
dwelling place for *all fullness of grace and all good.*
How can we not think here of the Annunciation
narrative (Lk 1:26–38) where the Father sends
his messenger to Mary *full of grace* and overshad-
ows her with the Holy Spirit so that she may
bear his Son who is the all good!

From the fact that Francis identifies Mary
with the Church, there is, in this text, a back and
forth movement from one to the other. What is
affirmed of Mary also applies to the Church and
reciprocally. The traits attributed to Mary can also
be found in the Church. Mary is an anticipatory
realization of the fullness which the Church will
be at the end of time. By calling Mary *Virgin made
Church*, Francis gives to both of them not only the
same titles, but considers their deep reality, their
ultimate mystery in the same way.

After this contemplation of the grandeur of
Mary, based on her bonds with the Triune God,
Francis uses poetry to express his admiration.
Six times, always beginning with the word *Ave,*

he will greet Mary with different names. The first three are related to the idea of a building. In turn Mary is a *palace*: a spacious and sumptuous edifice; a *tabernacle*: a holy tent in the desert and sheltering the ark of the covenant; a *dwelling*: a humble family home for daily living. She is also a *robe*: not only does she serve, like an edifice, as a shelter and a covering, but also as a garment for God, wrapping him with her humanity to protect and adorn him. The two final titles are traditional ones: *handmaid* and *mother*. *Handmaid* is the only name which Mary gives to herself in the narrative of the Annunciation (Lk 1:38) and in the song of the Magnificat (Lk 1:48). Others call her Lady and Queen; she only sees herself as a handmaid, that is her title of glory. The name of *mother* was first given to her by her cousin Elizabeth (Lk 1:43). It is because she is *the mother of my Lord that she is inundated with the fullness of grace* and that *the all good, the only Son, full of grace and truth* (Jn 1: 14) dwells in her.

This text — should one call it a prayer? — presents us with a tableau in which the *theotokos*, like the Church, it too Virgin, is enthroned but in the posture of a servant, while the Father, the Son and the Spirit consecrate and crown her. This is how *the pure heart* of Francis scrutinizes the humble and numinous depths of the mystery of Mary.

Bonded with her Son, with the Father, and with the Spirit, Mary, nonetheless, remains on

the side of "the immense throng of witnesses" of
which she is the center, as proven by the following
passage from the Earlier Rule:

> *Because of your love,*
> *we humbly beg*
> *the glorious Mother, the most blessed,*
>   *ever-virgin Mary,*
> *Blessed Michael, Gabriel, and Raphael*
> *all the choirs of the blessed*
> *seraphim, cherubim, thrones, dominations,*
> *principalities, powers, virtues,*
> *angels, archangels,*
> *Blessed John the Baptist*
> *John the Evangelist,*
> *Peter, Paul,*
> *the blessed patriarchs and prophets,*
> *the Innocents, apostles, evangelists, disciples,*
> *the martyrs, confessors and virgins,*
> *the blessed Elijah and Enoch,*
> *all the saints who were, who will be, and*
>   *who are*
> *to give You thanks ...*
> *as it pleases You*
> *God true and supreme,*
> *eternal and living,*
> *with Your most beloved Son,*
> *our Lord Jesus Christ,*
> *and the Holy Spirit, the Paraclete,*
> *world without end. Amen. Alleluia.*

> *(ER 23, 6)*

An "immense procession of all the saints" is evoked in this text. What is emphatically requested from it: *because of your love to give thanks* to the Father, the Son and the Paraclete. It is, to be sure, a rare petition. An awareness of the powerlessness of the human condition to sing God's praises appropriately imposes this recourse to the witnesses who have already attained true life and knowledge. Mary presides over this glorious celestial liturgy: celestial spirits encircle her and three of them carry proper names: Michael, Gabriel, Raphael; the others are regrouped in the "nine choirs" as designated in the Scriptures.

Among the saints, the first one to be named is John the Baptist, "the greatest among the sons of men," accompanied by the beloved disciple, John the Evangelist, and preceding here Peter and Paul, who, in the usual order, are mentioned first. Francis must have remembered his baptismal name which was John. What follows, in the order of the litany of saints, are the different categories which attempt to enumerate all the forms of Christian holiness, without forgetting the eternal dimension which unites the past to the future by the present: *who were, who will be, and who are.* Two unusual names are mentioned, *Elijah and Enoch,* thus evoking *the saints of the last days:* those who did not die (Gn 5:24; 2 Kings 2:11) will return at the end of time and those still in agony invoke them as witnesses of the life to come.

The contemplation of the mystery of Mary in God's plan has allowed us to better see the two dimensions of her life: on the one hand, her place in the depths of the Trinity and, on the other hand, in the midst of humankind. It is with her, the Mother of Jesus (Acts 1:11), that we are called to persevere in prayer, which is above all blessing, praise, and thanksgiving.

Reflection Questions

What is the place of Mary in your spiritual life? What is your favorite Marian feast or image and why? Is saying the rosary or Angelus part of your spiritual life? Is Mary a model of human liberation for you? What are the yeses, maybes and buts that interfere with acceptance of God's plan for your life? What are the family dynamics, church experiences and cultural influences that have helped shape your personal images of motherhood and of Mary? Male or female, what does it mean for you to mother God into this world and to become like Mary as a person and as Church?

11
Praised Be You in All Your Creatures

Focus Point

////////////

All of created reality sings the wonders, the beauties and grandeur of God. But it is only a heart that has been dispossessed and poor that can perceive the interdependency / connectedness of all created reality. It is only with such a liberated heart that one can truly see the world as "pregnant with God" (Angela of Foligno).

////////////

Most High, all-powerful, good Lord,
Yours are the praises, the glory, the honor,
  and all blessing.
To You alone, Most High, do they belong,
and no one is worthy to praise your name.

Praised be You, my Lord, with all Your
  creatures,

especially Sir Brother Sun,
Who is the day and through whom You
give us light.
And he is beautiful and radiant with great
splendor,
and bears a likeness of You, Most High One.

Praised be You, my Lord, through Sister
Moon and the stars,
in heaven you formed them clear and
precious and beautiful.

Praised be You, my Lord, through Brother
Wind,
and through the air, cloudy and serene,
and every kind of weather,
through whom You give sustenance to your
creatures.

Praised be you, my Lord, through Sister
Water,
who is very useful and humble and precious
and chaste.

Praised be You, my Lord, through Brother
Fire,
through whom You light the night
and he is beautiful and playful and robust
and strong.

Praised be you, my Lord, through our
Sister Mother Earth,
who sustains and governs us,

*and who produces various fruits with
    colored flowers and herbs.*

(CtC)

////////////////

A common cliché presents Francis as a
carefree vagabond, a musician and a
dancer. The *Canticle of the Creatures* would be
an expression of this levity. However, the most
ancient and trustworthy witnesses on the origins of this poem testify to its birth following a
dark night of the spirit.

We find ourselves in 1225, one year before
Francis' death. Francis is bed-ridden, almost
completely blind. At San Damiano, in the garden
of the monastery where he is received and cared
for by Clare, on a sleepless night, he has just
plummeted into the physical and psychic depths
of suffering. In a state of near final agony, as it
were, and filled with compassion upon himself,
writes his biographer, Francis turns to God in
prayer, and with a sudden burst of hope, opens
himself to the certitude of the life to come which
awaits him. The canticle which he will dictate at
that moment is a song which celebrates his victory over despair, a gaze, still tear-filled but also
appeased, at the beauty and the harmony which
God creates in the universe.

The title habitually given to the canticle
could be misleading and make us believe that

it has to do with singing the praises of created reality. The text, however, is totally turned towards God. With the exception of the final refrain, *praise and bless my Lord,* it is always God to whom the text refers and not creatures.

The *most high, all-powerful and good Lord* is invoked above all because of his supreme elevation, his distance: he is *Lord* (named ten times as such); to him alone belong *the praises, the glory, the honor, and all blessing.* He is the one whom creation must *praise, bless, give thanks, and serve with great humility.* We are always in an atmosphere of praise, the characteristic of most of Francis' texts when he speaks about God. The greatness of God, however, does not exclude his nearness and his proximity for he is *a good Lord.* Then, after having given four titles to the Lord, Francis, aware of the inaccessibility of God and the incapacity of human beings to grasp him by naming him, concludes with the affirmation: *No one is worthy to mention your name.* Boundaries are established here. Everything in creation and in human beings points towards God, speaks of him, and reveals him, but nothing could ever circumscribe him in a word, an image, or a concept. God is always beyond, further, and elsewhere.

It is to this transcendent God alone that *praise* is appropriate — for the unveiling of his manifestation in the world — in a wonder-filled and enthusiastic thanksgiving. For all creatures give us a glimpse of God's dazzling glory. Francis enumerates six elements which make up our universe. Day and night with their respective luminaries, the diurnal one — *the sun* — and the nocturnal ones — the *moon and the stars*; *the air* with its variables: the wind, the clouds, the serene sky; *water; fire; and earth* with its vegetation: herbs, flowers, fruits. The absence of animals is noteworthy. All these elements are placed together in three pairs and as alternately masculine and feminine.

These creatures are given, according to what their sex symbolizes, the names of *brother, sister, mother.* What stroke of genius we could ask gave Francis the intuition, the first one to do so in history, to discover a sort of parental linkage with inanimate beings? The terms brother-sister-mother not only suggest kinship and tenderness, but also imply the same matter and origin as basis for this rapport. The elements celebrated are, like us, constituted by the same mysterious matter and arise from the same creative impulse. Between ourselves and them there is not a radical discontinuity but rather mutual bonds that need to be highlighted.

In such a fashion, the beauty, the radiance and the splendor of *sir brother sun* are then described. His special rank is emphasized by the word *sir*: master, lord. Francis sees the sun as the primary symbol of the glory of God, of which *he bears likeness. The moon and the stars*, feminine figures which "console the dark realms of the night" (St. Augustine) are *clear, precious and beautiful*. If the *wind* does not receive any qualifiers, Francis, nonetheless, specifies the ongoing changes in the heavens: *air, clouds, serene skies*. As for *sister water,* she is like a young daughter, *very useful and humble and precious and chaste*. The beautiful *brother fire* irradiates the night with the joy that is emitted by *his robust and strong heart*. If our brother fire is called *sir*, our *sister, mother earth,* is also a nourishing *mother* whose fecundity: herbs, flowers, fruits, enables us to live and fills us with wonder.

> *Praised be you, my Lord, through those who*
> *   give pardon for Your love,*
> *and bear infirmity and tribulation.*
> *Blessed are those who endure in peace*
> *for by You, most high, shall they be crowned.*
>
> *Praised be you, my Lord, through our Sister*
> *   Bodily Death,*
> *from whom no one living can escape.*
> *Woe to those who die in mortal sin.*
> *Blessed are those whom death will find*
> *in Your most holy will,*
> *for the second death shall do them no harm.*
>
> *(CtC)*

These final verses of the canticle which follow the ones filled with wonder over the beauty of creation are in such contrast with one another! From the world of objects we switch to that of human beings. And not human beings in their beauty and strength but rather as wounded by offenses, affected by sickness and anxiety, handed over to the grips of death, *whom no one living can escape.* Facing the numinous harmony of things, and in opposition to it, a realm of negativity surfaces: human suffering and death, the inevitable culmination of earthly life. These two verses serve as good witnesses of the night journey traversed by Francis. It is from a wounded heart that a song of praise bursts forth. Only the revelation of love can enable one to *give a pardon for your love,* forget offenses, *and endure infirmity and tribulation in peace.* At the end of a hard and rocky road, the crown awaits with its victory trophy.

Death itself, tenderly called *Our Sister Bodily Death,* comes across as having been tamed. Since we cannot escape it, what we can do is enter into the obscurity of its mystery, abandon ourselves to the will of God with the guarantee that once the threshold is crossed, we will penetrate into a space where death is no longer: *for the second death shall do them no harm.* This is why, with the same movement as in what preceded in the text, Francis can praise God from a human passivity which has been assumed and leads into hope.

The numinous and glorious character of what is addressed in the first six verses suddenly becomes nocturnal. Human existence in its tragic dimension makes its appearance: the wounds which occur in relationships and which must be forgiven, sickness, anguish and death. But over and above this battlefield, a serene melody makes itself heard: it sings of love, forgiveness, peace, the crown of glory, and the holy will of God. Twice the word *happy* comes up as an echo of the Beatitude of those who are afflicted and persecuted.

The unity of this song with its contrasting harmonies comes from the different aspects of reality which are associated and reconciled. God manifests himself in the beauty of creation and in the midst of human darkness when it is assumed. We cannot dismiss either one. The praise of God can burst forth as much from contemplating the admirable order of creation as from the depths of human suffering when one can intuit and accept its hidden meaning.

It is to every situation that the invitation of the final verse can be applied:

> *Praise and bless my Lord*
> *and give Him thanks*
> *and serve Him with great humility.*

Reflection Questions

How do ecological issues such as global warming, famine, air quality and nuclear detonations affect the quality of your spiritual life and the survival of our planet? Is it easier to find God in the beauty and harmony of creation than it is in the suffering and struggles of our dark nights? In the sufferings of the poor, the dying, the hungry? As you ponder the beauty of creation, what does this mean for your spiritual life? "Beauty will save the world" (Dostoevsky), what does this mean for you? Of all the elements (earth, air, fire, water) which is the one to which you most relate? Is death a sister or a friend for you?

12

To See the Father and Christ through the Holy Spirit

Focus Point

////////////

Jesus is the paradigm of what it means to be fully human and the portal through whom we can discover the depths of God's life and love for us. It is only through the gift of the Spirit that the teachings of Jesus can live within us and grant us the freedom to serve others especially the most dispossessed. It is the same Spirit who enables us to truly believe that in the Eucharist we receive the body and blood of Jesus which makes us holy and fully alive.

////////////

The Lord Jesus says to his disciples:
I am the way, the truth and the life;
no one comes to the Father except through me.

If you knew me, you would also know my
  Father;
and from now on, you do know him and
  have seen him.
Philip says to him: Lord, show us the Father
and it will be enough for us.
Jesus says to him:
Have I been with you for so long a time
and you have not known me?
Philip, whoever sees me sees my Father as
well.

(Adm 1)

////////////

*T*his first Admonition can be considered as
a brief treatise on the knowledge of God
and of Jesus in his history and in the sacrament
of the Eucharist. This theologically dense text,
marked by a strong Johannine stamp, reveals
the roots of true knowledge.

It begins by a passage from John's gospel
(14:6–9) quoted in its entirety. To *know* the
Father, to *see* him, there is only one way: *the
Lord Jesus, the way, the truth and the life.* The four
verses are focused at once on the Father and on
the Son. It is the way of the Son which we must
adopt. He is the one whom we must know and
see. But the Son is only to be understood as a
reference to the Father: his face is not his own:
he is the face of the Father: *the one who sees me*

sees the Father. The Son does not substitute him-self for the Father nor does he replace him. By who he is, he reveals the Father.

> *The Father dwells in inaccessible light and*
> *God is spirit*
> *and no one has ever seen God.*
> *He cannot be seen, therefore, except in the*
> *Spirit*
> *because it is the Spirit that gives life,*
> *the flesh has nothing to offer.*
> *But because He is equal to the Father,*
> *the Son is not seen by anyone other than*
> *the Father*
> *or other than the Holy Spirit.*

(Adm 1)

The Father cannot be attained other than by the way of the Son: to know and see him is to see the Father. It might seem that the knowledge and the vision of the Son are easy to come by and are accessible, but this is not the case. "If you knew me," "you have not known me" are reproaches which Jesus addresses to Philip and his companions.

What follows in the text faces this difficulty and, far from resolving it, seems to plunge us deeper into it. By means of a combination of Pauline (1Tim 6:16) and Johannine texts (Jn 4:24; 1:18) what is affirmed is the *inaccessibil-ity* of the Father who *dwells in a dazzling light; no one has ever seen him*, for he is spirit, beyond the grasp of our intellect and our senses. As much as in the preceding passage the words *Father, to know, to see,* were preeminent, now it is the word *spirit* which is foremost. God the Father being spirit can only be seen in the spirit, who, unlike the flesh, alone can give life (Jn 6:64). In other words, the strictly human approach (*the flesh)* by the senses does not provide access to the mystery of the Father. An indefinable factor must come into play: breath, wind, a life which we call *spirit* and which the final sentence identifies with the person of the *Holy Spirit.*

All the more so that the Son himself, revealer of the Father and mediator for knowledge of him, is as inaccessible as the Father: *inasmuch as He is equal to the Father* (in his divine being), he is not *seen by anyone other than the Father.* We find ourselves on a road with a dead-end. The Father is invisible, only the Son can reveal him. But the Son himself, whom we thought we could humanly perceive, eludes, like the Father, our capacity to do so. *The Spirit* who makes vision possible is also invisible.

How can we resolve this dilemma which seems to exclude all knowledge of the mystery seen here in its Trinitarian dimension? Francis will not respond to this dilemma directly, but he will describe the path through which we can have access to a full vision of the Lord Jesus, either in his earthly condition or in his sacramental state.

All those who saw the Lord Jesus according to the humanity, therefore, and did not see and believe according to the Spirit and the Divinity that He is the true Son of God were condemned. Now in the same way, all those who see the sacrament sanctified by the words of the Lord upon the altar at the hands of the priest in the form of bread and wine, and who do not see and believe according to the Spirit and the Divinity that it is truly the Body and Blood of our Lord Jesus Christ, are condemned.

This is affirmed by the Most High Himself Who says: This is my Body and the Blood of my new covenant which will be shed for many; and whoever eats my flesh and drinks my blood has eternal life.

It is the Spirit of the Lord, therefore, that lives in its faithful that receives the Body and Blood of the Lord. All others who do not share in this same Spirit and presume to receive Him eat and drink judgment on themselves.

(Adm 1)

During the historical and earthly life of Jesus, his contemporaries could see his humanity concretely, but those who remained on this level, who did not get a glimpse, in the light of the Spirit, of the secret depths of his divinity, fell short of grasping the mystery of the Son. Strictly historical knowledge was useless to them.

Today, now that we no longer know Jesus according to the flesh (2 Cor 5:16), in his earthly condition, something analogous to this type of knowledge is provided for us: the sacrament of the Body and the Blood. As formerly, in his flesh and its historical manifestation, it is an empirical and very ordinary reality which is set before us: bread and wine, the ritual of the words and the presence of the priest.

The witnesses of the past were invited *to see and to believe* (to see and to believe in Johannine language means to come to Jesus, attain him on the level of faith). Similarly, believers of today must cast their gaze beyond the material elements and the rite. The words of *the Most High himself* attest to the deep reality of the Eucharist; *presence: this is my Body and the Blood of the covenant* (Mk 14:22, 24); *communion: who eats my flesh and drinks my blood enjoys eternal life* (Jn 6:54).

What follows is the key sentence of the Admonition and it responds in a certain way to all the questions raised until now by shedding light on all of them: *It is the Spirit of the Lord, therefore, that lives in its faithful that receives the Body and Blood of the Lord.*

Henceforth, the impasse is resolved. To be sure, the Father always dwells in inaccessible light and no human being can see him. The Son who alone reveals him also eludes a knowledge according to the flesh, whether in his earthly condition now forever in the past, or in his sacramental state, the only one we know. The Spirit, who is likewise *not seen by anyone other than the Father and the Son*, and lives, as a consequence, in a realm beyond our capacity to perceive him, *lives*, nonetheless, *in his faithful*. Invisible and inaccessible, he is the one who, strangely enough, enables us to see and experience, *according to the spirit and the divinity*, the secret reality of the Eucharist: the crucified and risen Lord. Dwelling in us, overshadowing us as over the Messiah (Is 11:2) and the Virgin Mary (Lk 1:35), he *receives*, by us, *the Body and Blood of the Lord*, that is to say, he helps us to detect (1 Cor 11:29) and recognize the living presence of the Crucified-Risen One in the elements and the ritual.

Francis then leaves these elevated thoughts for a more simple exhortation, but one that remains based on a very deep theological vision.

> *Therefore, children, how long will you be hard of heart? Why do you not know the truth and believe in the Son of God? Behold, each day He humbles Himself as when He came from the royal throne into the Virgin's womb; each day He Himself comes to us, appearing humbly; each day He comes down from the bosom of the Father upon the altar in the hands of a priest.*
>
> *(Adm 1)*

The Son of God is with us, even if no longer in the same way *"as in the days when He was in the flesh"* (Heb 5:7). If, rather than being pure and free, our hearts are heavily laden with concerns and worries, we risk letting the truth pass us by *and not know the Son of God.* All the more so that this glorious Son "who is in the bosom of the Father" (Jn 1:18) and who is seated "on a royal throne" (Wis 18:15) does not come to us in the dazzling glow of his majesty but *appears humbly* as a very ordinary daily food. He *humbles Himself,* as before when "He took flesh in the body of a virgin," and, leaving the bosom of the Father, he allows himself to be taken by human hands. Francis sees the Eucharist as a prolongation of the kenosis of the Servant. What the senses see of him is not even a human body, as humble and as hidden as it might be, but something very simple and almost insignificant. Such a manifestation of glory and hiddenness at the same time!

> *As He revealed Himself to the holy apostles in true flesh, so He reveals Himself to us now in sacred bread. And as they saw only His flesh by an insight of their flesh yet believed that He was God as they contemplated Him with their spiritual eyes, let us, as we see bread and wine with our bodily eyes, see and firmly believe that they are His most holy Body and Blood living and true.*
>
> *(Adm 1)*

Once we have grasped the spiritual path that Francis was describing in the first part of his text, the final lines are translucent. They sum up in one sentence the two states of Christ: his earthly life and his present sacramental status.

In this way the Lord is always with His
faithful, as He Himself says:
Behold I am with you until the end of the age.

Our circular movement is ended. "The way, the truth, and the life," by which we go to the Father is always with us (Mt 28:20). As the Spirit leads us to this path, revealing to us "the depths of God" (1 Cor 2:10), we commit ourselves to it with an expanded heart and, contemplating from afar the face of the Son, we discover that of the Father, "Who sees me also sees my Father."

Reflection Questions

Do you see a connection between the teachings of Jesus and your personal fulfillment? What are the specific questions of Jesus that most directly speak to you? What are the ones that are most costly for you to put into action or realize? Living out which one of the Beatitudes is most important in the world today? How has Jesus revealed himself to you broken and risen in your life and in those you encounter?

13

The Purest
Form of Praise

Focus Point

////////////

God reveals himself to us very personally, unveiling facets of who he is in different ways and at different moments throughout our lives. To be able to name these experiences and how they affect us is key to discovering our own unique identity. It is crucial that in order for this identity to unfold we do not attribute to God names that are not honest or that are someone else's names for God or impose on other people our names or image of God. Francis' "Praises of God" contains over 40 names for God. God is at once "unnamable and omninamable" (Eckhart).

////////////

You are holy, Lord,
You alone are the God
who does wonderful things.

You are strong. You are great.
You are the Most High.
You are the almighty king.
You are holy Father,
king of heaven and earth.

You are three and one, the Lord God of
*   gods;*
You are the good, all good,
the highest good.
Lord God living and true.

(PrsG)

///////////////

*T*his handwritten litany of pure praise which Francis scrawled on a small piece of parchment is preserved in the Basilica in Assisi. It was in September of 1224 and on Mount La Verna where he was spending a few weeks of solitude that an extraordinary event erupted in his life. He had just been marked with the stigmata of the Passion of Christ whom he had seen, crucified and glorious, in a mysterious vision. His favorite companion, Brother Leo, afflicted by a spiritual trial, wanted to have, for his consolation and peace of mind, something from Francis. It is this request that moved Francis to put into writing the praises which overflowed from his heart. Brother Leo received this piece of writing as a talisman and carried it on himself for the rest of his life.

What is initially striking in this text is that no allusion is made to the event of the stigmatization and its import. The orientation is Trinitarian with, as always for Francis, the presence of the *holy Father* at the center. Here again there is no petition, no act of thanksgiving, in short, no turning in on himself, but simply a pure gaze of wonderment at the splendor of the One on which it rests itself. The words are simple and burst out spontaneously one after the other. They arise nonetheless from deep experience and lengthy rumination.

Holiness, otherness and separation, is the first word: the majesty of *the Lord God* who *alone does wonderful things* is manifested. *The wonderful things* mentioned allude to Psalm 85:10 and concern all the merciful and wonderful interventions of God in the world. No doubt Francis includes the secret wonder that God has just accomplished in him by making him conformed to his crucified Son.

The attributes which follow: *strong, great, most high, all-powerful king, king of heaven and earth* all emphasize the grandiose dimension of the divine mystery: its strength, its elevation, its glorious and universal reign. The tender and respectful *holy Father* borrowed from Jesus' priestly prayer (Jn 17:11) of which Francis is especially fond — he refers to it ten times in his writings — tells us that this all-powerful God is also the father of Jesus Christ and our father.

Having called upon the Father, Francis sees him as he is in communion with the Son and the Holy Spirit; the Lord is, as has already been said, *Trinity and Unity*; an otherness and a difference both respected and affirmed but which, as it flows into Unity, do not separate or divide. The Lord is *God of gods* (Ps 135:2); all the values other than him, be they highest and made gods by human beings, are nonetheless subordinate to him for "he holds dominion over all the gods" (Ps 96:9). For God alone is *the highest good*: what satisfies, rejoices, and gives pleasure; that for which human beings are made; a happiness engendered by the possession of the good sought. He is also *every good*; for everything in him is good. And what exists as a good in creatures is but a trace, a reflection of the One who is the *highest good.* Reacting perhaps against these abstract terms which he had to use, Francis reaffirms the personal and warm character of the Lord God: *He is living and true.*

> *You are love, charity*
> *You are wisdom*
> *You are humility*
> *You are patience*
> *You are beauty*
> *You are meekness*
> *You are security*
> *You are rest*
> *You are gladness and joy*

You are our hope
You are justice
You are moderation
You are all our riches to sufficiency
You are beauty
You are mildness
You are the protector
You are our guardian and defender
You are strength
You are refreshment
You are our hope
You are our faith
You are our charity
You are all our sweetness
You are our eternal life.

(PrsG)

We are presented here with a litany of divine names: twenty-four times we hear these two words: *You are.* Francis has gone out of himself; he is indeed no longer himself and does not see anything else but the Other, the You, whose inexhaustible fullness of being he tries to suggest by repeated stammering. Is there a sequence, a logic in the twenty-seven different names he attributes to God? Humbly, in respect for this love poem, let us follow each of these expressions according to their place in the text and the associations they suggest.

You are love, charity: this is indeed the first name of God, the only definition, one could say, that Scripture gives him (1 Jn 4:16). To the biblical expression, *charity*, Francis adds, to form a couplet, the more current word *love*. Both proclaim that God is ecstasy, emptying of himself in his internal communion (Trinity) and in his Passion for the world, which he calls to, in men and women, to become his partner. The term *wisdom* has a more complex meaning. At once denoting life experience, capacity for judgment, a deeper view of reality, wisdom is also, as the etymology of the word suggests, savor, the taste that we find in the encounter with God. Is Francis the first one to call God *humility?* As elevated and glorious as he may be, God reveals himself as if he were hidden in the background and weak; he does not impose himself but discretely makes his presence known in silence. He is *patience* (Ps 70:5): the One who can keep holding on, lasts, and allows us to endure when suffering comes our way.

Beauty and *meekness* are placed together. Out of distraction? Or rather for the sake of emphasis, for Francis will repeat the same couplet later. The *beauty* of God consists in the splendor and the fascination which emanate from him and draw every contemplative gaze towards him. This beauty is not terrifying as it is accompanied by meekness (*mansuetudo*). God, in a way, accustoms himself to human beings and places himself on our level.

Security and rest are two ideas connected to one another. God alone is the shelter that can preserve us from all dangers and threats and in whom we can find calm and total rest. The effects are expressed by the following attributes: *joy, gladness, hope. Joy* is a dynamic manifestation of the experience of happiness; when it exteriorizes itself in festive song, it becomes *gladness* or jubilation. To the word *hope,* expectation of the promised happiness to come, Francis adds the possessive plural *our,* which will be repeated later, as if to emphasize that God does not exist for himself alone but also not only for me, but for all, for us. *Justice and moderation* (or temperance) evoke the two cardinal virtues to which will be annexed later on, God's *strength.* God is *justice,* the One who weighs everything according to their proper value; who knows what men and women are made of; and who does not, initially, manifest the rigor of his demands but rather his intention to love and to save. He grants his benefits and doles out the trials in proportion and as fitting to what each one can bear, according to *moderation.* This moderation or right measure is only outdone by his love which is without moderation or measure! God is, finally, *all our riches.* Francis, the poor man and the singer of poverty, knows that what is lacking in our human condition will fade away to make place for the infinite superabundance of God.

After the repetition of the couplet *beauty* and *meekness* which, in any case, whether it is a lapsus or a voluntary repetition, emphasizes the importance that these values have for Francis, four terms express the notion of protection based on strength: *protector, guardian, defender, strength*. Like a strong man, God protects (a maternal gesture) and defends (warrior-like); he is also like a shepherd who guards his flock. One can trust him because vigor and strength are not found wanting in him.

As in what preceded in the prayer where security and rest engendered joy, here, the assurance of protection produces *refreshment*, a word which evokes an energizing, joyful, and festive meal among friends.

The five final terms are all accompanied by the possessive *our.* Francis, in his prayer, intentionally speaks in the name of a community. He applies to God the name of the three theological virtues: *you are our hope, you are our faith, you are our charity. Hope*, contrary to the usual order, comes first. It is God who is this wonderful happiness which everything in us longs for and calls upon. He is *our faith;* his light enlightens our darkness and allows us to see what true reality consists of, what lies beyond the surface and appearances. And for the second time *charity* is said of God: in the depths of his being there is nothing else but love; it is this love alone which, in turn, enables us to love others.

Because this is so (that God is love) to sum up the entire prayer Francis uses words that are more and more all-encompassing: *You are our sweetness, our eternal life.* This word "sweetness" is perhaps the one that best expresses Francis' subjective experience, his taste of God, and about which he is always reticent to mention.

> *Great and wonderful Lord,*
> *Almighty God, merciful Savior.*

The final verse repeats some of the adjectives already utilized: *great, almighty*, and adds two others: *wonderful, merciful*. The all-powerful and great Lord God cannot but stir up, in the one who experiences it, a movement of adoration. The final word is more tender: everything culminates and is recollected in the infinite mercy of the One who did not come to condemn but to save: *merciful Lord* (perhaps the only allusion to Jesus).

Muslim piety has a litany of 99 names attributed to God drawn from the Koran and proposed to the ruminations of the believer. Francis' *The Praises of God* contains 43, and counting the repetitions, 60. These names invite us to leave our own turmoil and place the gaze of a pure heart on the One who is:

> *Almighty God, merciful Savior.*

Reflection Questions

What are the names of God in your own life and experience? Have these names evolved over time? Can you identify moments when there was an important shift in the name you used to pray to God. What is your personal favorite at the moment? How does it affect your sense of self? What is your least favorite way to name God? Are there names that you find painful that touch a wounded part of who you are? Is there a name that you would like to pray to God with but cannot at the present moment? And why?

14
Let Us Desire Nothing Else

Focus Point

////////////

Desire is a key to the spiritual journey. Too often, however, our desires are entangled with that which is trivial and don't grant us ultimate satisfaction. The consumer culture that we live in is built on the lure of false and empty objects of desire. The redemptive strategy of God is to deepen our desires and transform them into yearning for God so we may cry out "my soul is yearning for the living God." We will not encounter our true self until we attend to and befriend our deepest desires and find true rest in God.

////////////

With our whole heart,
our whole soul,

our whole mind,
with our whole strength and fortitude,
with all our powers,
with every effort,
every affection,
every feeling,
every desire and wish,
let us all love the Lord God
Who has given and gives to each of us
our whole body, our whole soul and our
    whole life,
Who has created, redeemed and will save us
by his mercy alone
who did and does everything good for us,
miserable and wretched,
rotten and foul,
ungrateful and evil ones.

(ER 23, 8)

//////////////

*I*n this final section of the Earlier Rule, addressed to men and women of all times, we are all summoned to the love of God. What is entailed is to discover how God has loved us and what are the ramifications of this love. Using it as a starting point, we are called upon, by a concentration of all the dynamisms of our being, to manifest our gratitude, which is our way of loving.

How, then, does this love of *the Lord God* manifest itself to men and women? *He has given and gives to each one of us our whole body, our whole soul and our whole life.* Francis acknowledges that the first gift, the basis for all the others, is the gift of existence, one made up of body, soul, and life. We cannot accuse him of dualism or of despising the body: it is because of the gift of the body and the soul that he gives thanks. Like his sister Clare, he can sing: *Blessed are you for having created me!* The same grateful acknowledgment is, then, repeated in a more theological language: God *has created, redeemed us* by restoring his creation, damaged by sin, and leading it to *salvation*, its final destiny. Aware that men and women cannot attain total fulfillment either by their own strength, or by their works, Francis adds: *only God's mercy* assures us of salvation. It is, however, as if the recalling of these basic gifts of God — life, redemption, salvation promised and assured — did not suffice for Francis and that he needs, afterwards, to show that God's love for men and women is unconditional by insisting on the misery of human beings and their failure to be grateful. God did do good and does not cease from doing good to us *who are miserable and wretched, rotten and foul, ungrateful and evil ones.* This emphasis on the corruption of human beings surprises and even startles us. It is true that this emphasis is inserted here as a rhetorical device to emphasize the contrast with the absolute character of the love of God which extends itself to the unlovable and even the repulsive. We need to notice, nonetheless, that out of the six terms being used, four are biblical citations. *Miserable and wretched* (Rv 3:17), *ungrateful and evil* (Lk 6:35) do in fact describe the human condition as God sees it, which does not preclude the fact that he is good towards it. The odorous terms, *rotten and foul,* do come from Francis and are found elsewhere in his writings (ER 22, 6; 2LtF 46). He uses them to express the disgust which can arise in men and women when they become aware of their rottenness.

God is not egotistical and closed up within his own beatitude. He is the One who *gives* and *does good* not only to those who do not deserve it, but even to those who are clearly unworthy. To discover this awakens the hearts of human beings, who are created for and *to be towards God,* as St. Augustine puts it, and moves them to thanksgiving, which is a prelude for and a way to love. Taking up again the commandment of love (Dt 6:5; Mk 12:30), Francis will insist on the intensity of this love which is meant to carry and to lead human beings and their entire make-up towards this God who is so good. To the six spiritual energies mentioned in Scripture: *heart, soul, mind* (the spiritual components of the person), *strength, fortitude, powers* (the vigor with which these components must express themselves), he adds, on his own, six others: *understanding, effort, will* (something voluntaristic in the last two), *affection, feeling, desires* (three expressions of human affectivity). So that while he seems to discredit human beings as *miserable and wretched,* he acknowledges, on the other hand, the extraordinary riches which are in them and which they can use in their search for God.

Ultimately, this text is a song which sings the glory of the unconditional love of God and also proclaims the grandeur and the dignity of human beings capable of opening themselves to be receptive to such a love.

> *Therefore,*
> *let us desire nothing else,*
> *let us want nothing else*
> *let nothing else please us and cause us*
> *   delight*
> *except our Creator, Redeemer and Savior,*
> *the only true God,*
> *Who is the fullness of good,*
> *all good, every good, the true and supreme*
> *   good,*
> *Who alone is good,*
> *merciful, gentle, delectable, and sweet,*
> *Who alone is holy,*
> *just, true, holy, and upright,*
> *Who alone is kind, innocent, pure,*
> *from Whom, through Whom and in Whom*
> *is all pardon, all grace, all glory*
> *of all penitents and just ones,*
> *of all the blessed rejoicing together in heaven.*
>
> *(ER 23, 9)*

Francis presses us to want and to desire God alone, and nothing else. *To want and to desire* mean that we turn ourselves completely and with our deepest longings towards the One who is the only *pleasure* and the only *delight* that can satisfy us totally. These four words: *want, desire, please, delight,* whose importance is accentuated by the expression *nothing else*, suggest that in the hearts of men and women there exists a wounded and an unfulfilled desire that John of the Cross calls a "sweet cautery." The only reality that can heal this wounded desire, the only true pleasure and eternal delight is God himself. To say who God is for men and women Francis will accumulate, as in *The Praises of God* (meditation for the thirteenth day), a series of adjectives each of which will try to suggest an aspect of God's being. What is highlighted, first of all, is God's goodness. Six different aspects of this goodness, which are also synonyms, hardly suffice to describe it. God is *the fullness of good*, for whom nothing is lacking; he is *all good*, outside of which there is no good that exists; *every good*, because everything in him is good; *true and supreme good,* because nothing in him is illusory, deceptive, and above which no other being can be conceived; *Who alone is good*, because he is the prototype and the source of every good outside of him. Was Francis aware of all these meanings, or did he content himself, in a sort of poetic frenzy, simply to align words next to one another?

After this very general, almost abstract attribute, there are four others, with a more affective connotation and drawn from the realm of human relationships, which are related to God. Like a friend or, perhaps, a spouse, he is *merciful, gentle, delectable, and sweet.* From this human realm we move to an aspect with greater gravity: only God is *holy*, that is to say different and separate; *just*, because he sees and appreciates reality according to its just merits; *true,* because in him there are no false or misleading appearances; *upright*, because he is true, he is honest and loyal. An alternating movement makes us return to divine *kindness* (or forbearance), then to two qualifiers which may surprise us. God, for Francis, is *innocent* and *pure.* An allusion, perhaps, to the eternal and abyssal youthfulness of God, always in the process of being born....

The passage which follows is more articulated theologically. It describes the relationships which exist between the different categories of men and women, whether they be still alive or dead. Human beings, now, are being envisioned according to three situations: as *penitents:* those who commit themselves to ongoing conversion; as *just ones,* those who, already transformed and purified, persevere in their journey toward God; as *blessed rejoicing together in heaven,* those who celebrate the joy of communion with God. For the penitents God is *all pardon;* for the just ones, *gracious forbearance;* for the blessed, *resplendent glory.*

Thus, for everyone, God engulfs everything and immerses it into an unfathomable ocean of immense joy and perpetual festivity. We understand better now that, compared to this discovery, everything else loses interest, can no longer be absolutized, and can only serve, at the most, as an approach to the mystery. The *nothing* which is so often repeated (as the *nada* of John of the Cross) means that separated from God, reality is empty and deceptive, that it even becomes an obstacle, a wall of separation, and a shield. Thus

> *let nothing hinder us,*
> *nothing separate us,*
> *nothing come between us.*

> *(ER 23, 10)*

It has often been said, in too facile a way, that, contrary to John of the Cross, who preaches a radical detachment from creatures, Francis indicates a way to God through creation. The opposition between the two is artificial; in any case, what precedes obviously shows that, for Francis, a certain egotistical if not idolatrous approach to creation hinders the encounter with God.

> *Wherever we are,*
> *in every place,*
> *at every hour,*
> *at every moment of the day,*
> *every day and continually,*

let all of us truly and humbly believe,
hold in our heart and love,
honor, adore, serve,
praise and bless,
glorify and exalt,
magnify and give thanks
to the Most High and Supreme Eternal God
Trinity and Unity,
Father, Son and Holy Spirit,
Creator of all,
Savior of all
who believe and hope in Him,
and love Him, Who,
without beginning and end,
is unchangeable, invisible,
indescribable, ineffable,
incomprehensible, unfathomable,
blessed, praiseworthy,
glorious, exalted,
sublime, most high,
gentle, lovable, delightful,
and totally desirable above all else
for ever. Amen

(ER 23, 11)

God is good to men and women and he lavishes them with his gifts. Independently of these gifts, he is in himself lovable and delightful. He remains, nonetheless, eternally incomprehensible and *no one is worthy to mention his name.*

What we can do, as human beings, is to praise and exalt him. The third summons, which reaches us like a big wave, pulls us into the ultimate depths of the mystery of God's being. The terms already encountered elsewhere: *most high, supreme and eternal God, Trinity and Unity, Father, Son, Spirit, Creator and Savior* designate this mystery using names drawn from the Christian tradition. Those who, with faith, hope, and love, hand themselves over to God know and do not know who he is. Francis, who uses an abundance of words (eighty-six in his writings) to name God, has recourse here to what theology refers to as apophatic or negative language. God is *invisible* to human eyes; *incomprehensible* and *unfathomable,* beyond our capacity to grasp him intellectually; *indescribable* and *ineffable,* beyond words to describe him. In relationship to the human experience of duration and time, God is also, *without beginning and end,* incapable of variation, *unchangeable.* What then can we say about the One who is *glorious, sublime, most high, exalted,* if not that he is *blessed and praiseworthy?* Before such unfathomable depths what is appropriate and imposes itself more and more is awe-filled wonder, the unceasing proclamation of the beauty of God, which the language of the Scriptures and the liturgy calls adoration, blessing, and praise. Let us *praise and bless, glorify and exalt, magnify and give thanks* — such is the doxological attitude that Francis proposes in his customary manner of celebrating God. But even if praise — the pleasure of speaking about God — takes on more importance for Francis, he will also speak of faith as a humble remembrance in the heart: *let us truly and humbly believe and hold in our hearts;* of *love,* and of *service*, as obedience to God's word; and of the reverence due to the mystery: *let us honor and adore.*

Finally, after having seemingly relegated God to a realm "beyond all created reality," Francis ends with a remembrance of the supreme beatitude that the experience of God brings to men and women. This God is

> *gentle, lovable, delightful*
> *and totally desirable above all else*
> *for ever. Amen.*

Reflection Questions

What are some of the false and empty objects of desire that trap you? Make a list of consumer goods and advertising that prey upon your superficial desires. Are there any desires that have become compulsive for you and addictive — money, gambling, computer usage, smoking, sex, etc.? What is the relationship that you see between your sexual desires and your passion for God?

15
Rendering
Everything to God

Focus Point

At the heart of the Christian life is the awareness that everything comes from God and from his Spirit. Only a heart that is pure and completely dispossessed can acknowledge simultaneously that God is the source of every good and be able to render everything to God in an act of perfect praise and thanksgiving. A lifelong commitment to become and end up truly poor deepens and liberates the inner space for God to fully manifest himself. It creates correspondingly the totally free person capable of singing God's praise in humble and joyful adoration, a fitting climax to the journey of Francis of Assisi, the poor man who sang God's praises.

Let us refer all good
to the Lord, God Almighty and Most High,
acknowledge that every good is His,
and thank Him,
from Whom all good comes,
for everything.
May He, the Almighty and Most High,
the only true God,
have, be given, and receive
all honor and respect,
all praise and blessing,
all thanks and glory,
to Whom all good belongs
He Who alone is good.

(ER 17, 17-18)

///////////////

*T*he text which precedes plays on two key
expressions: *all good; refer and acknowledge.*
As elsewhere in Francis' prayers, the center of
the text is *the Lord God Almighty and Most High,*
the only true God to whom all good belongs; from
Whom all good comes, Who alone is good. In fact,
as Jesus declared in the Gospel (Lk 18:19), God
alone is good. Everything which human beings
call good or goodness exists fully only in him.
Life, intelligence, love, communion, beauty, festivity, sweetness, order, harmony, serenity, joy
— all these qualities fundamentally and above
all belong to God. When we find manifestations

of them in creation — and we do so continually — they always flow from the unique source, *from which all good comes.*

Francis' very pressing invitation moves us to take the two following steps. First of all, *acknowledge* the sovereign and unique goodness of God as he is in himself and in the very depths of his being. Then, *acknowledge* his presence in all of creation: in men and women and their activity in history and in the world of things; in short, in all of his works, "which, in passing, he has adorned with his beauty" (John of the Cross). This supposes an eye and a spirit that are awake, attentive, benevolent; and which discover traces everywhere of the One *who alone is good;* and are filled with wonder and rejoice over it.

This act of acknowledgment will immediately be followed by one of letting go. We must *render,* relate to God what belongs to him alone. If he reveals to us the goods which are in him, or rather the Good that he is, this is cause for wonder for us but does not belong to us. For this revelation is a gratuitous gift, a grace. As is, even more, the kindness which he so profusely extends outside of himself and towards all his created reality. To be sure, we must acknowledge this goodness, admire it and rejoice over it like a child receiving a gift. But rather than claiming it for ourselves and considering it as our property, we must *render* it back to and present ourselves before the Giver in order to express our joy-filled thanksgiving for his generosity, thus rendering *back to Him the grace* we have received.

We now can better understand why Francis insists so much: *have, be given, and receive,* as well as the reason for the three couplets which follow. *Honor and respect*: that is to say, the reverence and the adoration of those who have received a glimpse of who God is; *praise and blessing*: the songs of wonder and tribute for who he is and what he does; *thanks and glory*: what God has given graciously is rendered back to him in thanksgiving for the praise of his glory.

> *In the love that is God, therefore, I beg all*
>   *my brothers ...*
> *to strive to humble themselves in everything,*
> *not to boast or delight in themselves*
> *or inwardly exalt themselves because of the*
>   *good words or deeds*
> *or, for that matter, because of any good that*
>   *God says or does*
> *or at times works in and through them.*
>   *(ER 17, 5-6)*

To dispossess ourselves joyfully and in praise from all the goods received from God by acknowledging that they do not come from us and do not belong to us — this is true poverty. Knowing the human heart — and first of all his own — Francis is aware that such an act of dispossession does not come by itself and his exhortation here attests to this difficulty.

He notices first of all that *good* can be found
in every human being. Elsewhere, he has celebrated the excellence of human beings as
images of God according to the spirit and the
body and made for the blessedness of eternal
life (Adm 1) and to whom God, in his gratuitous
love, *gives all his body, all his life* (ER 23, 8). Here he
sees an expression of the fundamental goodness
of the person manifesting itself *in the good words
and deeds*. Human speech and behavior can be
just, good, and in conformity with the truth of the
Gospel. But this fundamental and true goodness
which men and women discover in themselves
is a gift and a work of God. He is the One *who
says or does or at times works in and through them*.
With finesse, Francis distinguishes between the
good accomplished *in them* and *by them*. When
the power of the Gospel takes hold of men and
women, when their hearts change and gradually
turn towards God and the neighbor, when they
die to their naive egotism, then holy righteous-
ness and kindness become visible in them. They
come across as holy, near to God and like him.
The kindness of the new being which they have
become will radiate around them; through *the
good words and deeds* they will touch, influence and
perhaps transform those whom they meet. The
just person, the saint, is in some way contagious.

But such a situation, one similar to the condition of Adam and Eve in paradise, and given
the freedom of human beings and the depths of

their desires, entails a terrible risk: the supreme temptation of the just. It consists in *boasting or delighting in themselves or inwardly exalting themselves because of the good* that they discover in themselves as if they were the absolute owners of it. In Admonition 8, Francis, using two scriptural texts, discloses the mechanics of this temptation.

> *The apostle says: No one can say: "Jesus is Lord," except in the Holy Spirit (1 Co 12:3); and: "There is not one who does good, not even one" (Ps 13:3; Rm 3:12).*

This is a temptation which consists in two types of forgetfulness. A forgetfulness that everything comes from God and from his Spirit, especially when the very heart of Christian life is at stake: to confess the divinity of Christ. A forgetfulness, afterwards, of the radical incapacity of human beings, left to themselves, of doing any good whatsoever. These two quotations from the apostle Paul give us a glimpse of the extent to which Francis was marked by the Pauline vision of the human condition. With Paul he clearly grasped that the heart of radical Christian poverty consists in acknowledging that when humans are cut off from God they are incapable of doing any good and capable of doing every evil. Only the total handing over of ourselves to the loving mercy of God opens the way to salvation which is freely given.

We cannot better conclude these fifteen days spent with Francis than with another one of his prayers, one which serves as an ending to an invitation to worship God, a final cry, a total going out of himself in pure praise.

> *All-powerful, most holy, most high,*
>   *supreme God:*
> *all good, supreme good, totally good.*
> *You Who alone are good,*
> *may we give You all praise, all glory, all*
>   *thanks,*
> *all honor, all blessing and all good.*
> *So be it! So be it! Amen.*
>
>   *(PrsG 11)*

This is the total Francis, the true poor man, not above all of an outer poverty, but one emptied of himself, stripped of every claim to ownership, every pretense, even every virtue and as if completely taken up by the goodness and the holiness of what has seized him. The only response possible is the freedom chant of the one who, because he has nothing left of himself, possesses everything of this God, who, also poor himself, hands himself over totally to human beings.

Reflection Questions

What are the gifts you have received that make it easy for you to praise and give thanks to God? What do you perceive in what is going on in the world that lifts up your spirit in similar praise and thanksgiving? What blocks or obstacles do you see in yourself and in the world that prevents you for giving praise to God? Do you ever get angry at God? In what ways does our culture threaten to devalue the giftedness of your life? What in Francis' message have you found most liberating?

Bibliography

Francis of Assisi: Early Documents, The Saint, The Founder, The Prophet, eds. R. Armstrong, J. A. Hellmann, W. Short, 3 vols. (New York: New City Press, 1999–2001).

Brunette, Pierre, O.F.M. *Francis of Assisi and His Conversions.* Translated by Paul Lachance, O.F.M., and Kathryn Krug. Quincy, Il.: Franciscan Press, 1997.

Cunningham, Lawrence S., *Francis of Assisi: Performing the Gospel Life.* Grand Rapids, Michigan: William B. Eerdmans Publishing Company, 2004.

Leclerc, Eloi, O.F.M. *Wisdom of the Poverello.* Translated by Marie-Louise Johnson, M.D. Chicago: Franciscan Herald Press, 1961.

Manselli, Raoul. *St. Francis of Assisi.* Translated by Paul Duggan. Chicago: Franciscan Herald Press, 1988.

Matura, Thaddée, O.F.M. *Francis of Assisi, Writer and Spiritual Master.* Translated by Paul Lachance, O.F. M. with the collaboration of Colette Wisnewski. Cincinnati, Ohio: St. Anthony Messenger Press, 2005.

Also available in the
"15 Days of Prayer" series:

Saint Augustine *(Jaime García)*
978-0-7648-0655-6, paper

Saint Benedict *(André Gozier)*
978-1-56548-304-0, paper

Saint Bernadette of Lourdes *(François Vayne)*
978-1-56548-314-9, paper

Saint Bernard *(Emery Pierre-Yves)*
978-0764-805745, paper

Dietrich Bonhoeffer *(Matthieu Arnold)*
978-1-56548-311-8, paper

Saint Catherine of Siena *(Chantal van der*
    Plancke and Andrè Knockaert)
978-156548-310-1, paper

Pierre Teilhard de Chardin *(André Dupleix)*
978-0764-804908, paper

The Curé of Ars *(Pierre Blanc)*
978-0764-807138, paper

Saint Dominic *(Alain Quilici)*
978-0764-807169, paper

Saint Katharine Drexel *(Leo Luke Marcello)*
978-0764-809231, paper

Don Bosco *(Robert Schiele)*
978-0764-807121, paper

Charles de Foucauld *(Michael Lafon)*
978-0764-804892, paper

Saint Francis de Sales *(Claude Morel)*
978-0764-805752, paper

Saint John of the Cross *(Constant Tonnelier)*
978-0764-806544, paper

Saint Eugene de Mazenod *(Bernard Dullier)*
978-1-56548-320-0, paper

Saint Louis de Montfort *(Veronica Pinardon)*
978-0764-807152, paper

Henri Nouwen *(Robert Waldron)*
978-1-56548-324-8, paper

**Saint Martín de Porres: A Saint of the
Americas** *(Brian J. Pierce)*
978-0764-812163, paper

Meister Eckhart *(André Gozier)*
978-0764-806520, paper

Thomas Merton *(André Gozier)*
978-0764-804915, paper

Saint Elizabeth Ann Seton *(Betty Ann McNeil)*
978-0764-808418, paper

Johannes Tauler *(André Pinet)*
978-0764-806537, paper

Saint Teresa of Ávila *(Jean Abiven)*
978-0764-805738, paper

Saint Thomas Aquinas *(André Pinet)*
978-0764-806568, paper